The grace of the Spirit is truly necessary if we want to deal with the Holy Spirit; not that we may speak adequately about Him —for that is impossible—but that we may pass through this subject without danger, by saying what the divine Scriptures contain.

Cyrillus of Jerusalem, *Catecheses*, XVI, 1

Contents

Preface

This book contains the Annie Kinkead Warfield Lectures of the year 1964, which I had the great honor to give at Princeton Theological Seminary, February 3-7. I would like to thank the faculty of this world-famous center of theological thinking for the confidence which it has put in me and for its willingness to hear me speak on the work of the Holy Spirit. This theme, almost more than any other, causes a feeling of deep embarrassment in the mind of a theologian who dares to ponder it. We realize that we deal with things which are far beyond our understanding. Should we not limit ourselves to an act of adoration and gratitude, saying: "Thanks be to God for his inexpressible gift!" (2 Cor. 9:15)? Can we express ourselves on the inexpressible?

Asking myself these questions during the months of preparation, I shrank back several times from the task I had undertaken, even to such an extent that I was about to propose another theme to the faculty. But no—I could not let go the theme because the theme did not let go me. The feeling of embarrassment did not leave me, but it was more and more accompanied by the conviction that theology must not be silent about God's inexpressible gift. All God's deeds are inexpressible. We can dishonor them all by speaking about them in an irreverent way. But all God's deeds want to be confessed, in spite of—no, on account of—their inexpressibility. God wants us to love him with all our mind and with all our strength. True theology is an act of love. In this act we cannot be silent about a single one of God's mighty inexpressible deeds.

There is a special reason not to be silent about the work of

9

the Holy Spirit. Many Christians who like to speak about creation, incarnation, atonement, Christ, the church, and even the future, avoid speaking about the work of the Holy Spirit. In their opinion this work is so much a hidden, personal, and individual work that every attempt to formulate it in terms of theology would be an act of irreverence. Often the same persons like to speak about it in terms of personal experience, which they consider to be something widely different from theology. The result is a spiritual under-nourishment of theology and, as a consequence, of preaching, teaching, and church life, whereas religious groups which have an anti-theological sentiment appropriate the Holy Spirit for their private feelings.

This may be an overstatement in regard to the Anglo-Saxon world. At any rate there is a much richer literature on the work of the Holy Spirit in the English language than there is in the languages of the European continent. I gladly express my gratitude for what I owe to this literature. (Often it increased my reluctance to lecture in English on this theme. It seemed to me like carrying coals to Newcastle.) However, even here most literature on the Holy Spirit is of a devotional or semi-theological nature. More-over, many new insights in the field of biblical theology with regard to the Holy Spirit have not yet found their way to systematic theology, let alone to the pulpit and the life of the church. The efforts of many theologians are needed to fill what is still more or less a vacuum in the dogmatics of the contemporary churches.

It is true, beyond a doubt, that pneumatology is a neglected field of systematic theology. There are deep reasons for this. One of the deepest reasons lies in the nature of the Spirit itself. ". . . the Spirit . . . will guide you into all the truth; for he will not speak on his own authority . . ." (John 16:13). The Spirit constantly leads our attention away from himself to Jesus Christ. So he hides himself, on the one hand, in Christ; and, on the other hand, he hides himself in his operations in the life of the church and the lives of individuals. As a consequence, the Spirit is rarely mentioned in most of the confessions and in most of the dogmatical hand-books. He is spoken of in an often rather speculative way in connection with the Trinity. In the classical creeds, he is mentioned in one sentence after many sentences about Christ. The following sentences about the church, the forgiveness of sins, etc., can be understood as a description of the Spirit's actions, but he is no longer referred to explicitly. In the handbooks little attention, if any, is given to the connection of the Spirit, on the one hand, and the church, justification, sanctification, etc., on the other hand.

There are also historical reasons for this neglect of the Spirit. The enthusiasts of all ages—the Montanists, the Anabaptists, the Quakers, the Pentecostals, and many other movements which emphasized the presence of the Spirit—discouraged the official churches because they feared a loosening of the ties between the Spirit and the historical Christ, or between the Spirit and the letter of the Scriptures, or between the Spirit and the institutional church life.

This situation continued under other names in the nineteenth-century controversy between liberalism and orthodoxy, in which liberalism presented a new spiritualism which was rejected by orthodoxy because the liberal "spirit" seemed to be a mere extension of the human spirit, without the necessary christocentric outlook. For that reason the orthodox renewal after the First World War gave a new emphasis to Christology, largely at the cost of the interest in the working of the Spirit here and now.

So we live with an unhappy and sterile alternative, the bad consequences of which do not fail to materialize. On the one hand, we see the established larger churches which are unwilling to focus their attention on the action of the Holy Spirit; in their midst faith is in danger of becoming something intellectual, traditional, and institutional. On the other hand, we see the rapidly increasing Pentecostal movements, where the reality of the Spirit is often sought in the emotional, individualistic, and extravagant. Both parts live by the lacks and mistakes of the other, which give them a good pretext not to see their own lacks and mistakes, or the biblical truth represented by the other.

There are additional reasons for focusing our theological interest on the doctrine of the Holy Spirit. In the ecumenical discussions, we are again and again confronted with pneumatological questions. In regard to the Roman Catholic Church, many old controversial issues seem to lose their relevance; the remaining problems, in my opinion, all point to the nature of Christ's presence here and now, i.e., to the nature of the work of the Holy Spirit. The coming encounter with the Eastern Orthodox Church, which rejects the procession of the Spirit from the Son (the *filioque*), will also urge us to new and clear pneumatological insights.

It would be easy to extend the list of reasons for a new reflection on the work of the Holy Spirit. The deepest and most decisive reason, however, is the fact that the church by her very nature is *reformanda quia reformata*. Her continuity is realized in a steady renewal. Renewal (different from reorganization) is the work of the Holy Spirit; it is his answer to the prayer: Come, Creator Spirit! We cannot expect the necessary renewal without first having an awareness of the necessity of the Holy Spirit; and we cannot be aware of this necessity without knowing about his nature, his promises, his action, his gifts. Here we find the deepest reason why true theology, which desires to serve the church, never can cease to think of God's inexpressible gift in the Holy Spirit.

These lectures are being given in the same year in which the 19th General Council of the World Alliance of Reformed Churches will meet (in Frankfurt on Main) under the theme "Come, Creator Spirit!" I hope that these lectures may contribute to the spiritual preparation for this great Reformed meeting; and, even more, that the meeting itself may become a sign of the renewing presence of the Spirit and a source of new prayer and inspiration.

I

THE SPIRIT AND CHRIST

In trying to discover the real meaning of a word, we cannot depend too much on its etymology. The primitive meaning may have lost its power in the course of an age-long usage. The etymology of the biblical words for "spirit" is still transparent in the theological use. Both the Hebrew word *ruach* and the Greek word *pneuma* (as well as the Latin words *animus, anima, spiritus*) point to the movement of the air. According to the context, they can often be translated as "wind," "storm," "breeze," etc. More often, however, they point to the movement of the air which is caused by the breath, so that the meaning shifts to "breath," and in a more metaphorical way, to "principle of life," or "vitality." This holds true especially for the Hebrew word *ruach*, which is often connected with additional words like "*ruach* of sadness," "*ruach* of wrath," etc. Animals have *ruach*; men have *ruach*; God pre-eminently has *ruach*. He is a breathing, living, acting God. It is the great miracle of creation that this God transmits his *ruach* to his creatures and, in the highest degree, to man. ". . . God . . . breathed into his nostrils the breath of life; and man became a living being" (Gen. 2:7). Where God works, the air is stirred, *ruach* is at work. The primitive meaning of the word is transparent everywhere in the Old Testament. It is even still undecided whether in Genesis 1:2 we have to translate: "the Spirit of God was moving over the face of the waters" or "a heavy storm was blowing over the face of the waters."

In the Greek New Testament, the situation is basically the same. *Pneuma* is the act of blowing or breathing, and especially the sign, as well as the principle, of man's vitality. The Greek language has two words for the human spirit. One is *nous*, which is primarily the principle of man's theoretical faculties and which can often be translated as "mind" or "intellect." The other word is *pneuma*, which expresses the dynamic principle of life, man as a center of vitality and activity. In spite of the metaphorical and even philosophical significance which the word *pneuma* had received in Greek long before the time of the New Testament, its usage in the New Testament shows clearly its Old Testament background. We think of John 3:8: "The wind blows [*pneuma pnei*] where it wills . . . so it is with every one who is born of the Spirit [*pneuma*]." In John 20:22, we read that Jesus breathed on the disciples (Nestle mentions, in the margin, Genesis 2:7!) and said to them: "Receive the Holy Spirit"; we are almost inclined to translate, according to the context: "Receive the vivifying air current." A similar example occurs in the story of Pentecost, where "a sound came from heaven like the rush of a mighty wind," a *pnoe*, as a consequence of which the Apostles were filled with the *pneuma* (Acts 2:2-4).

"Spirit" means that God is a vital God, who grants vitality to his creation. Man's *ruach/pneuma* is the vivifying gift of God, on which man is entirely dependent. Therefore, I would propose this preliminary definition of the Spirit: It is God's inspiring breath by which he grants life in creation and re-creation. F. W. Dillistone defines it briefly: "*God in action in human life.*"[1] Even more distinct and meaningful are the words used by Alan Richardson to describe the nature of the Spirit: "The [*pneuma*] of a man is his [*dynamis*], his person in action; and the same is true of God's [*pneuma*]. . . . God's Spirit is God acting."[2]

"GOD IS SPIRIT"

In the context of this treatise, we cannot go into a description of the development of the concept of Spirit in the different stages of the Old Testament and of the New Testament. Suffice it to say that in the prophetic traditions of the Old Testament the faithful remnant is looking forward—out of the failure of Israel as God's elected partner—to the moment, in the last days, when God himself will make his partner act in accordance with his will. Through the prophet Jeremiah, he said: "I will put my law within them, and I will write it upon their hearts" (31:33). Or, as it reads in Ezekiel 36:26-27: "I will take out of your flesh the heart of stone and give you a heart of flesh. And I will put my spirit within you, and cause you to walk in my statutes and be careful to observe my ordinances." In the famous 37th chapter of Ezekiel, Israel in its sin and frustration is presented as a collection of dry bones. God says: "I will cause *ruach* to enter you and you shall live" (verse 5); "and I will put my *ruach* within you, and you shall live" (verse 14). Both the K.J.V. and the R.S.V. translate *ruach* in verse 5 as "breath" and in verse 14 as "Spirit." After what we heard about etymology, we can understand their problem but need not follow their solution. Ezekiel sees that in the last days God will perform a new creative act, similar to what he did to Adam. He will grant a new vitality to a people which is dead through trespasses and sins. The eschatological gift of the Spirit means the miracle of re-creation and regeneration of the chosen but disobedient people. Some in Israel already have God's breath, God's inspiring presence: Moses, some judges, some kings, and sometimes the prophets. That is not enough by far, however, to fulfill God's purpose for Israel. Therefore, ". . . it shall come to pass afterward, that I will pour out my spirit on all flesh . . ." (Joel 2:28).

In the mysterious figure of the Servant of the Lord, we see a prophecy of that great future: "Behold my servant . . . I have put my Spirit upon him" (Isa. 42:1). We hear it also in the voice which speaks in Isaiah 61:1-2: "The Spirit of the Lord GOD is upon me, because the LORD has anointed me to bring good tidings to the afflicted . . . to proclaim the year of the LORD's favor . . ." In these and other passages, we hear the expectation that the pouring out of the Spirit on all flesh will happen through the medium of one who is able to act as the true partner in the covenant with God, who is able to represent God to the people and the people to God. No wonder that in some prophetic passages this role is ascribed to the figure of the newly anointed, righteous King, the Messiah. "There shall come forth a shoot from the stump of Jesse, and a branch shall grow out of his roots. And the Spirit of the LORD shall rest upon him . . ." (Isa. 11:1-2).

With this background, we can understand what the New Testament says about the Spirit. Now that the last days have set in, the Messiah as the great bearer of the Spirit has appeared, and the pouring out of the Spirit on all flesh has begun. In the encounter of Jesus with the Samaritan woman, we hear what all this means. The woman speaks about the different places where Samaritans and Jews worship God. She wants to know which place is the right one. Jesus accepts her way of putting the problem as right for the time being. He says: The Jews are right, the Samaritans are wrong. But he says also: "Woman, believe me, the hour is coming when neither on this mountain nor in Jerusalem will you worship the Father. . . . the hour is coming, and now is, when the true worshipers will worship the Father in spirit and truth, for such the Father seeks to worship him. God is spirit, and those who worship him must worship in spirit and truth" (John 4:21, 23-24). "God is spirit"—much misunderstood and abused words. Generally they are understood as meaning: God is not bound to a special place of revelation; he is a spirit, invisible and omnipresent, beyond time and space, whom every man can find, if he retires into the depths of his own heart. The next verse, however, shows that the Samaritan woman had an entirely different idea of what Jesus meant. She said: "I know that Messiah is coming." She did not conceive of the word "spirit" in the modern sense of idealistic philosophy, but in the Old Testament sense. God is *ruach*: He is breathing the breath of life into man, that is, he is present, active, granting a new vitality. "And those who worship him must worship him in his *ruach*" (i.e., there where his active presence is at work) "and truth" (i.e., in his *emet*, his faithfulness to his covenant, his acting according to the promises which he gave through his prophets, that in the last days the Spirit, through the Messiah, will be poured out on all flesh). That hour is now. Now God can be worshiped in his *ruach* and his *emet*, in his promised vivifying presence. And the woman said: "I know that Messiah is coming."

Karl Barth's comment on this passage is: ". . . the opposite of Rome, Wittenberg, Geneva and Canterbury—is not the universe at large, which is the superficial interpretation of Liberalism, but Jesus."[3] And Dr. George S. Hendry expresses the same idea in this way: "The point, then, is not that locality has ceased to have any relevance to worship . . . The meaning is that the location has been redefined, and God is now to be worshiped in the place where he is present, i.e., in Him who is the truth incarnate . . ."4 Jesus Christ means: the real presence of God as Spirit in his indwelling and re-creating activity.

THE DOUBLE RELATION BETWEEN THE SPIRIT AND CHRIST

From what has just been said, we can easily understand that the relation between the Spirit and Christ in the New Testament is presented in two ways. The first one is dominant in the Synoptic Gospels. It describes the Spirit as having divine priority over against Jesus and Jesus as the bearer of the Spirit. This description is in accordance with the prophecies that the Spirit will rest on the Messiah. That is why he is called Messiah, the Anointed One, because the Lord has anointed him with his Spirit. According to Matthew and Luke, this resting of the Spirit on Jesus began with his birth, "for that which is conceived in her is of the Holy Spirit" (Matt. 1:20). The baptism by John in the waters of the Jordan, however, meant a new affirmation and revelation of the spiritual secret of Jesus' life. The Spirit came descending upon him like a dove, as the Spirit in the beginning was moving over the face of the waters of chaos, as the dove foretold to Noah the new creation out of the waters of judgment. "Then [the story goes on] Jesus was led up by the Spirit into the wilderness to be tempted by the devil" (Matt. 4:1). After the temptation, "Jesus returned in the power of the Spirit into Galilee" (Luke 4:14). In the same power he did his work; he cast out demons by the Spirit of God (Matt. 12:28). He rejoiced in the Holy Spirit (Luke 10:21) about the great events which happened through his work. Through the same Spirit, he gave commandment to his Apostles after the resurrection (Acts 1:2). So, in the words of Peter, the hearers can be reminded of the well-known fact of "how God anointed Jesus of Nazareth with the Holy Spirit and with power" (Acts 10:38).

This aspect, as we said, is dominant in the Synoptic Gospels. But it is not absent in Paul and John either. Paul writes, e.g., that

Jesus was "designated Son of God in power according to the Spirit of holiness by his resurrection from the dead" (Rom. 1:4); and John says that "it is not by measure that he gives the Spirit" to him whom he has sent (John 3:34).

In Paul and John, however, another relation between the Spirit and Christ is dominant. Here Jesus is not so much the bearer of the Spirit as he is the sender of the Spirit. Paul even says that Christ "became life-giving Spirit." He describes the Spirit as the Spirit of Christ or the Spirit of the Son (Rom. 8:9; 2 Cor. 3:17; Gal. 4:6; Phil. 1:19). John puts this relation in even clearer and stronger words. Here Christ speaks of the Spirit "whom the Father will send in my name" (John 14:26), and: "if I go, I will send him [the Counselor] to you" (16:7), "whom I shall send to you from the Father" (15:26). In John 20:22 the risen Christ, by breathing on his Apostles, transmits to them the Holy Spirit. This aspect, so dominant in Paul and John, is not absent in the Synoptic Gospels and in Acts. "And behold [we read in Luke 24:49], I send the promise of my Father upon you"; and in Peter's sermon on the day of Pentecost: "Being therefore exalted at the right hand of God, and having received from the Father the promise of the Holy Spirit, he has poured out this which you see and hear" (Acts 2:33).

These two aspects are by no means contradictory. On the contrary, they are complementary. We even find them together in one sentence in John 1:33, where God says to John the Baptist: "He on whom you see the Spirit descend and remain, this is he who baptizes with the Holy Spirit." Jesus can be the sender of the Spirit only because he is first the receiver and the bearer of the Spirit. Now in the tradition of the church and its theology, the first relation is very much neglected. That fact is understandable insofar as this relation is often abused by those who want to emphasize Jesus' humanity at the cost of his divinity. From the time of the Adoptionists at the end of the second century until the Liberals of our time, there is an inclination to see Jesus mainly or exclusively as the one who, in the line of the prophets and of all true children of God, though more than all of them, is gifted with the Spirit. The church, in reaction against that trend of thought, neglected this aspect and stressed, in an equally one-sided way, the fact that Jesus has the Spirit at his disposal and that it is his gift to his church.

Both aspects belong together, however, as is easily understood when we see Jesus Christ against the background of the promises of the Old Testament. From that perspective he is neither a purely divine person nor an ordinary human individual. He is (to use H. Wheeler Robinson's well-known expression) a "corporate personality." The whole of Israel and even the whole of mankind is summarized in him who is the Servant of the Lord, the Messiah, the Son of Man, the last Adam. All these names point to his function as our representative before God, as the true partner in the covenant, who acts and obeys so differently from us, but at the same time on behalf of us. "The LORD . . . saw that there was no man and wondered that there was no one to intervene" (Isa. 59:15-16). So his life-giving Spirit went out to a new creative act, to the creation of him who, in contrast to Adam, is the true "image of the invisible God, the first-born of all creation" (Col. 1:15). He is in a unique way conceived by the Spirit, guided by the Spirit, filled with the Spirit. In him God creates and becomes the partner that he did not find in mankind nor in Israel. And now he who is anointed with the active presence of God makes his decisions on behalf of Israel and of mankind. In this One, we the many are included. And when he as the One has completed his work, a new work has to begin: The blessing of his representative work has to come down to those for whom it has been done, who from the beginning were meant and included in his corporate personality. So the movement must be from the One to the many. Jesus is the great *pars pro toto*. Therefore, the movement now has to be from the *pars* to the *totum*. That is the second work of God's Spirit, of his active life-giving presence. First he creates the One; then he includes the many in the One. The Spirit rests on Jesus and the Spirit goes out from Jesus. He on whom the Spirit remains, this is he who baptizes with the Holy Spirit.

All this leads us to the conclusion that it is possible and even obvious to design Christology from a pneumatological viewpoint, that is, to conceive the person and the work of Jesus Christ as the result and the starting point, as the center of God's life-giving presence, of the work of the Spirit among men. Nevertheless, attempts to design such a pneumatic Christology are very rare in the history of theology. I suppose this is mainly due to the fear of Adoptionism.

It is not the dominating concept of the Spirit as such, however, which leads to Adoptionism, but the neglect of the strictly unique way in which the Spirit is united with Christ.

It is a remarkable thing that the first attempts in the fields of Christology were in the direction of a pneumatic Christology, as we see in the writings of the so-called "Apostolic Fathers." Ignatius calls Christ, according to his divine nature, *pneumatikos* (Epistle to the Ephesians 7,2), and he says that the faithful "possess the inseparable Spirit, who is Jesus Christ."[5] Second Clement to the Corinthians speaks of Christ "who, being first Spirit, became flesh."[6] We find the most famous, though often misunderstood, example of this pneumatic Christology, in the Fifth Parable of the Shepherd of Hermas. There, as in the former quotations, it is the Spirit which is incarnated in Christ. The most striking passage reads: "God made the Holy Spirit which existed before and which created the whole creation, dwell in a flesh which He elected. Now this flesh, in which the Holy Spirit dwelt, served the Spirit well in a behaviour of purity and virtue, without casting any stain on the Spirit." For that reason, the passage goes on, the flesh (i.e., the human nature of Christ), after his earthly work, was exalted and elected to the fellowship of the Spirit.[7]

Around the middle of the second century, these features of a pneumatological approach to Christology died away. An echo is yet heard in Tatianus' "Speech Against the Greeks" (around A.D. 165), which speaks of "the heavenly word, born as Spirit from the Father and as Word out of his rational power."[8] This expression is typical for the transition which now takes place. The Word instead of the Spirit becames the principle of incarnation. For Tatianus they are yet one, in a good Old Testament way, because: "By the word of the LORD the heavens were made, and all their host by the breath [or the spirit] of his mouth" (Ps. 33:6). *Ruach* and *dabar* are almost synonymous. That knowledge was soon forgotten, however. The Logos was a popular philosophical concept of that time. The Christian apologists preferred it as their christological cornerstone, because it made the gospel acceptable to their intellectual contemporaries. So the pneumatic Christology was replaced by the Logos-Christology and soon forgotten. The Logos-Christology however, just because of its philosophical connotations, caused a distortion in the presentation of the gospel. It took the church two centuries at least to remove the bad consequences of the mixture of biblical teaching and Hellenistic cosmology. One can defend the thesis that even today the trinitarian dogma, born out of the Logos-Christology, still bears the marks of that mixture, at any rate in some speculative and even tritheistic aspects which are inherent in its traditional presentation. We must ask the question whether a radical return to a pneumatic Christology would not do more justice to the biblical message, and be more relevant to the modern mind, than our traditional categories. It is clear that such a rethinking would not leave the trinitarian dogma unaffected. In the course of this book we shall several times have the opportunity to come back to these fundamental problems.

THE SPIRIT AS THE ACTION OF THE EXALTED CHRIST

So far our main interest has been focused on the consequences of Christ's being the bearer of the Spirit, and as such also the sender. Now we have to shift our attention and to lay full emphasis on that second aspect: Christ the sender of the Spirit, the Spirit sent by Christ. How are Christ and the Spirit related here? This difficult question is of the greatest importance. It has found different answers in the course of church history, and these answers have created different types of Christian life, institutional as well as individual.

For the sake of surveyability in this complicated field, we start by comparing the two main types of Christian life. The first type is well known and even dominant in our Reformed tradition. It conceives of the relation of the sending Christ and the sent Spirit in such a way that the Spirit is strictly subjected to the historic Christ and has, as its task, to apply the salvation obtained by Christ to mankind. This conception can refer to many well-known scriptural passages, primarily to the words of the departing Jesus in John 14-16, e.g., "the Holy Spirit . . . will . . . bring to your remembrance all that I have said to you" (14:26), "he will bear witness to me"

(15:26), "he will not speak on his own authority . . . He will glorify me, for he will take what is mine and declare it to you" (16:13-14). The beloved Pauline words in this connection are: "no one can say 'Jesus is Lord,' except by the Holy Spirit" (1 Cor. 12:3). The work of Jesus is the content of the Spirit's work. On the day of Pentecost the Spirit moves Peter to prophesy, not about the Spirit, however, but about what happened to Jesus. "For the testimony of Jesus is the spirit of prophecy" (Rev. 19:10).

One can say that this is the main trend in pneumatology in the great Christian tradition. It belongs also to the heritage of the Reformed church. I will use two examples: Calvin and Barth. Warfield was the first to characterize Calvin as the theologian of the Holy Spirit, and rightly so. The famous third book of the *Institutes* contains great riches in the field of pneumatology, many of which have not yet been uncovered by the Reformed churches. In many ways Calvin transcends the antitheses which I have to draw here, especially in his doctrine of the union with Christ. His starting point and his main trend, however, are in line with what occupies us here. The superscription of the first chapter of the third book reads: "The Things Spoken Concerning Christ Profit Us by the Secret Working of the Spirit." And the first two sentences say: "We must examine this question. How do we receive those benefits which the Father bestowed on his only-begotten Son—not for Christ's own private use, but that he might enrich poor and needy men?" Near the end of the first paragraph, Calvin summarizes the work of the Spirit in these words: ". . . the Holy Spirit is the bond by which Christ effectually unites us to himself."[9]

The same tendency is found in Barth's *Church Dogmatics*, especially in the volumes I-IV, 1. I draw your attention particularly to I, 2, § 16, of which the first section is entitled: "The Holy Spirit the Subjective Reality of Revelation," a title which corresponds to that of § 13, 1: "Jesus Christ the Objective Reality of Revelation." The Spirit is the power of the application of God's revelation in Christ. Many years later we find the same trend in IV, 1, § 62, 1, "The Work of the Holy Spirit." Just one characteristic quotation from this section: "But fundamentally and generally there is no more to say of Him than that He is the power of Jesus Christ in

which it takes place that there are men who can and must find and
see that He is theirs and they are His . . ."[10]

It would be an easy thing to heap up quotations of this kind.
This is the main pneumatological trend in ecclesiastical theology.
The Spirit is customarily treated in noetical, applicative, subjective
terms. He is that power which directs our attention to Christ and
opens our eyes to his work. The main result of his work is the
awakening of faith in Christ. His work is merely instrumental. He
himself wants to step back and to remain hidden in order to give
way to the encounter between Christ and man. So the Spirit is a
second reality beside Christ, but entirely subordinate to him, serving in the application of his atoning work, in the realization of
justification by faith.

But does this presentation of pneumatology do full justice to
the preaching of the New Testament about the Spirit? There are
good reasons for denying this. The Spirit is far more than an instrumental entity, the subjective reverse of Christ's work. His coming
to us is a great new event in the series of God's saving acts. He
creates a world of his own, a world of conversion, experience, sanctification; of tongues, prophecy, and miracles; of mission; of upbuilding and guiding the church, etc. He appoints ministers; he
organizes; he illumines, inspires, and sustains; he intercedes for the
saints and helps them in their weaknesses; he searches everything,
even the depths of God; he guides into all truth; he grants a variety
of gifts; he convinces the world; he declares the things that are to
come. In short, as the Johannine Jesus says: "he who believes in me
will also do the works that I do; and greater works than these will
he do, because I go to the Father" (14:12).

These and similar words were in the minds of all those who, in
every century of church history, protested against the lack of spiritual reality in the official church life, and who did so in the name
of the New Testament promises about the activity and the gifts
of the Spirit. We think of the groups already mentioned in the
Introduction, from the Montanists of the second century to the
Liberals, on the one hand, and the Pentecostals of the twentieth
century, on the other hand. In spite of their varieties and contrasts,
they have in common that they, as over against the official churches,

consider the Holy Spirit as an independent reality with his own content. Here he is not only instrumental to Christ, but he is also a center of new actions. He is not so much to be understood in noetical and applicative terms as in ontological and creative terms.

The biblical basis for these spiritualistic countercurrents is evident. Their biblical weakness is not less evident, however. They, in their turn, cannot do justice to the intimate connection of the Spirit with Christ. To them the Spirit is more or less emancipated from Christ. To the same extent he is mainly connected with the religious individual. The difference between God's Spirit and man's spirit is in danger of becoming blurred, for the same reason that Christ, as the sole center and object of faith, vanishes gradually and turns into a historic initiator or a religious principle. Here we observe the danger of a fading away of the christological substance, as we observed the danger of a petrification of that substance in the former group. Here we feel the threat of individualistic subjectivity, as there the threat of institutional objectivity. We can repeat what we said in the Introduction: Both parts live by the lacks and mistakes of the other.

The urgent question rises about whether we can overcome this sterile antithesis. I believe that it is possible. In the field of biblical theology, several studies have been published in the last years which throw a new light on the relation between the Spirit and Christ, primarily in the letters of Paul.[11] From these studies and from an open-minded examination of the New Testament, we must draw the conclusion that we have to think of the Spirit in strictly christocentric terms. This means that we have to start where the first group starts and to say that the Spirit is always and everywhere the Spirit of Jesus Christ.

When we go a step beyond the traditional position, it is not to weaken it but to strengthen it. That the Spirit is bound to Christ is far more true than is meant and expressed in classical pneumatology. In John 14:18, Jesus, aiming at the sending of the Spirit, says: "I will not leave you desolate; I will come to you." We find a parallel saying in the last words of Matthew: "I am with you always, to the close of the age" (28:20). This identification of the Spirit with Christ is found in all the New Testament traditions.

We think of 1 John 3:24 which says that we know Christ abides in us "by the Spirit which he has given us." In the letters to the seven churches, it is the risen Christ who speaks, but who at the same time says: "He who has an ear, let him hear what the Spirit says to the churches" (Rev. 2:7, etc.). We think, however, mainly of Paul's words: "Now the Lord is the Spirit" (2 Cor. 3:17a). Some think that we have to reverse subject and predicate, and to translate: "Now the Spirit is Lord," the Spirit wields lordship; but the word "Lord" in verses 17 and 18 always means Christ. He himself is the Spirit; as the close of verse 18 repeats: "this comes from the Lord who is the Spirit." Other features of this conception in Paul are found in 1 Corinthians 6:17: "he who is united to the Lord becomes one Spirit with him," and in Romans 8:9-11, where the divine principle which dwells in the faithful alternately is called the Spirit, the Spirit of God, the Spirit of Christ, and Christ. It is also clear that the Pauline expressions *en Christoi* and *en pneumati* are synonymous. In his study *Kyrios and Pneuma*, Ingo Herrmann, in particular, draws our attention to what he calls the "identity-expressions" in Paul. His conclusion is: "that Paul answers the question of the relation between Kyrios and Pneuma in the sense of identity."[12] An even more striking formulation, which Herrmann gives in view of 2 Corinthians 3:17, is this: "Pneuma is a functionary concept (*Funktionsbegriff*): it is the divine power by which the exalted Lord as the possessor of the Pneuma is present and active in his Church"; and: "This Pneuma is the Kyrios Christ himself, in as far as he gives himself to man and can be experienced by man."[13] These words remind us of the words which we quoted before from Alan Richardson, who considers *pneuma* as the predicate of a subject, or as a function: "The [*pneuma*] of a man is his [*dynamis*], his person in action." Ingo Herrmann, as a good Roman Catholic, feels that these results are not in harmony with the traditional trinitarian dogma which describes the Spirit as a separate person beside the Son; he nevertheless sticks to his exegetical findings, and rightly so. The trinitarian consequence of this view, which is in accordance with the Old Testament concept of Spirit, will have to occupy us at a later stage.

If we are right in saying that Christ and the Spirit are identical

and that the Spirit is Christ in action, we go far beyond the traditional connection between Christ and the Spirit. Moreover we as-
sociate both in a way which is different from the tradition. The
tradition says that the Spirit opens our eyes for the person and work
of Jesus Christ; it thinks mainly of incarnation and atonement. The
traditional Reformed sermon, as instrument of the Spirit, attempts
to open the eyes of its hearers to their being lost and to the necessity, as well as to the reality, of the justification of the sinner by
Christ's blood. Earlier, I quoted the opening sentences of Calvin's
pneumatology. Let me now quote the third sentence: "First, we
must understand that as long as Christ remains outside of us, and
we are separated from him, all that he has suffered and done for
the salvation of the human race remains useless and of no value
for us."[14] I want to point to the words "all that he has suffered and
done for the salvation of the human race"; these words show that
the relevance of Christ's sacrifice for our justification is the main
purpose of the Holy Spirit. Calvin's few words can stand for an
age-long tradition.

Here also biblical theology has brought a renewal, which is the
consequence of the discovery of the identity between Christ and
the Spirit. This is not a complete identity. Christ, as the risen and
exalted Lord, is the Spirit. Before, the Spirit was, so to speak, his
private possession, not his function. As John 7:39 expresses it: "for
as yet the Spirit had not been given, because Jesus was not yet
glorified." The reverse of this fact is what Paul says: "the last Adam
became a life-giving spirit" (i.e., through his resurrection; 1 Cor.
15:45). In John it is the resurrected Jesus who breathes on his disciples to give them the Spirit. Paul expresses this connection of the
Spirit and the resurrection several times. He speaks of "the Spirit
of him who raised Jesus from the dead" as dwelling in the faithful
(Rom. 8:11), and he says that our walking "in newness of life" is
a result of the fact that "Christ was raised from the dead" (Rom.
6:4). We think also of how, in the story of Pentecost (Acts 2), the
risen Christ is the center of Peter's sermon and how "this which
you see and hear" is ascribed to Jesus "being . . . exalted at the right
hand of God" (2:33). Käsemann—in his article on the Spirit in the
New Testament in R.G.G.³—rightly says, particularly in view of
Paul's utterances: "This means that the Spirit is the earthly pres-

ence of the exalted Lord. To say it more precisely: 'in the Spirit the Resurrected One is manifested in his resurrection-power.' "[15] The Spirit is the new way of existence and action by Jesus Christ. Through his resurrection he becomes a person in action, continuing and making effective on a world-wide scale what he began in his earthly life.

Here the question must arise, What is the exalted Lord aiming at in his new manifestation as Spirit? The answer is included in what we said earlier about Jesus as a corporate personality. Being our Representative, he has to do a twofold work. On the one hand, he has to do as *pars pro toto* what the *totum* is unable and unwilling to do. That he did in his obedience, his sacrifice, and his resurrection—once-for-all and as the one-for-all. And now, having put to death the old man, our own sinful existence, and having received and become the new man in his resurrection, he has to implant this new reality into the old mankind, he has to go from the *pars* to the *totum*. That is what he does as Spirit, and we understand now why the Spirit could not be given, in the proper and full sense of the word, before Jesus was glorified.

Now it can be clear what the purpose of the Spirit is. Christ as life-giving Spirit wants to take men into his fellowship in order that they may partake in and be transformed into the new humanity which he has obtained for us. Generally we define this purpose in terms of justification. We then say that the Spirit convinces us that Christ's sacrifice is our righteousness and that through faith in his Word we stand before God as the new man. That is right. That is the first half of the incorporation of the many into the One. It is fundamental; it is not the end, however; it is the root, but not the fruit. The ultimate end, as Paul formulates it, of Christ's becoming a life-giving Spirit is: "Just as we have borne the image of the man of dust, we shall also bear the image of the man of heaven" (1 Cor. 15:49). God's last goal is not justification but sanctification and even glorification. Christ will change our lowly existence to be like his glorious existence, conformed to the new manhood of his resurrection (cf. Phil. 3:21). So Christ's risen and exalted human nature is not only the starting point but also the goal of his spiritual activity. The new shape (*morphe*) of the One is the beginning; the *symmorphia* of the many is the end. "For those whom he

foreknew, he also predestined to be conformed to the image of his
Son, in order that he might be the first-born among many brethren"
(Rom. 8:29). And so "we all . . . beholding the glory of the Lord,
are being changed into his likeness" and "this comes from the Lord
who is the Spirit" (2 Cor. 3:18). Or, to use the words with which
Ingo Herrmann summarizes the tendency of 2 Corinthians 3: "The
pneumatical Lord because of his presence changes man towards
himself, in a developing process, and so makes him participate in
the Spirit and the Glory of God."[16]

Before concluding this chapter, we have yet to face a difficult
question: How do we have to conceive of this identity of the Spirit
with the exalted Lord? Traditional theology would avoid the word
"identity" or merely speak of an identity in functions of the Son
and the Spirit. This position is untenable, however, if we face the
fact that the Spirit in Scriptures is not an autonomous substance,
but a predicate to the substance God and to the substance Christ.
It describes the fact and the way of functioning of both.

Nevertheless, we cannot take the opposite position either, by
saying that the Spirit is merely another name for the exalted Christ.
In that case we would forget that the New Testament knows about
difference as well as about identity. The same Johannine Jesus who
says, "I will not leave you desolate; I will come to you" (14:18),
also says: "the Father . . . will give you another Counselor" (14:16).
Paul also sometimes distinguishes between the operations of Christ
and those of the Spirit, e.g., between "the grace of the Lord Jesus
Christ" and "the fellowship of the Holy Spirit" (2 Cor. 13:14).
And in Revelation 22:17, we read that the Spirit together with the
church is praying to the exalted Christ: "Come." We think also
of expressions like "the Spirit of Christ," "the Spirit of his Son."
I understand all these words in such a way that they express the
conviction that the risen Lord transcends his own functioning as
life-giving Spirit. He is eternally in the glory of the Father as the
first fruits of mankind, as the guarantee of our future, as the advo-
cate of his church. His life, as the life of the One in which the goal
of humanity is attained, is more than his function toward us. At the
same time we must say, however, that the word "function" is too
weak in this context. Christ's movement toward us is not a mere
action but his entrance into us in a special *modus existendi*, the

mode of immanence, in which he nevertheless does not cease to remain transcendent as the exalted Lord.[17]

Our considerations seem to be rather far removed from the traditional approach. This fact should not be exaggerated, however. It would not be difficult to quote corresponding trends of thought, e.g., from Calvin.[18] I will confine myself to the well-known words in Answer 86 of the Heidelberg Catechism, where the question of why we must do good works is answered in this way: "Because just as Christ has redeemed us with his blood he also renews us through his Holy Spirit according to his own image." Here Christ himself is the subject of the Spirit and his aim is conformity to his image.

In the nineteenth century, the older and the younger Blumhardt were the two great pastors and thinkers for whom these insights were a reality. They experienced the living Christ as present and active himself in his Spirit, achieving his creative work of conversion, healing, and sanctification. At the end of the struggle with the possessed Gottliebin Dittus, the demon in her cried with a loud voice: "Jesus is conqueror!" These words, for Johann Christoph Blumhardt, became the characteristic of the age of the Spirit in which we live now. For him the Spirit is the risen and mighty Lord Jesus.

In a more theological way this insight is expressed in the last volumes of Barth's *Church Dogmatics*. We mentioned him before as a spokesman of the traditional view. Suddenly we find a deepening and widening of his view in § 64, 4, called "The Direction of the Son," where he speaks about the Spirit as the power of Christ's resurrection, which works the miracles of light, liberation, knowledge, peace, and life (even healing). Here Barth defines the Spirit as "no other than the presence and action of Jesus Christ Himself: His stretched-out arm; He Himself in the power of His resurrection, i.e., in the power of His revelation as it begins in and with the power of His resurrection and continues its work from this point."[19]

Along this line—the Spirit as the risen Christ, reaching out to the *totum*, to conform us to his image—we hope to attain a synthesis between the traditional and the spiritualistic types of pneumatology. Whether this is the right way, the working out of this approach in the next chapters will have to show.

II

THE SPIRIT AND THE MISSION

According to the usual order found in dogmatics, we now expect a chapter about Word and Spirit, about the Spirit and the individual, or about the Spirit and the church. None of these subjects can be seen in the right perspective, however, without a previous consideration of the mission as the first and basic act of the risen Christ. Neither the church nor the regenerated individual would exist without first having missionary witness. If it be true, as we said before, that the Spirit is the movement of the representative One to the represented many, it is likewise true that the fundamental shape of this movement is the mission, which for this reason has a logical priority in the order of the pneumatical acts.

PRIORITY OF THE MISSION

One can object that mission, in its turn, cannot be thought of without a preceding community of the church or a preceding witnessing faithful individual. So the logical priority of the mission seems to be doubtful. We find a continuous interaction, so that systematically we move within a closed circle. However true this may be, the circle, though not having a starting point within itself, has an origin from outside. It is created by the active presence of Christ. It is the result of his movement, of his sending action. Both the church as a community of men and the mission as an activity of men are the result of the creative missionary action of the Spirit. "As the Father has sent me, even so I send you" (John 20:21).

Christ's mission is first; church and mission are its interacting results.

For that reason we cannot speak of the chronological priority of the mission, but we must speak of its logical priority. This priority is reflected in the striking fact that, whereas in the Gospels the church plays a minor role, the mission is dominant in the description of the activity of the risen Christ. We think of the closing passages of all four Gospels. Matthew speaks about the missionary commandment: "Go therefore and make disciples of all nations"; for the fulfillment of this commandment Christ promises his active presence: "I am with you always" (28:19-20). In the enlarged ending of Mark, we find the same commandment with the closing words: "And they went forth and preached everywhere, while the Lord worked with them and confirmed the message by the signs that attended it" (16:20). A shorter version of the ending (also included in the r.s.v.) reads: "And after this, Jesus himself sent out by means of them, from east to west, the sacred and imperishable proclamation of eternal salvation." The end of Luke simply mentions the words: "I send the promise of my Father upon you" (24:49), but the beginning of Acts gives a more elaborate form: "But you shall receive power when the Holy Spirit has come upon you; and you shall be my witnesses in Jerusalem and in all Judea and Samaria and to the end of the earth" (1:8). Finally, John tells us that Jesus said: "'As the Father has sent me, even so I send you.' And when he had said this, he breathed on them, and said to them, 'Receive the Holy Spirit'" (20:21-22). We can also mention the missionary context of John 21, which begins with the miraculous draught of fish as a parable of the coming miracle of the mission. In all these stories we find three striking facts: (1) the absence of the church (the more remarkable according to the laws of the *Formgeschichte,* since the primitive church easily could have retroprojected its existence and importance into these stories!), (2) the dominance of the mission, (3) and the promise of the Spirit as the power and the guide in that great new event. There is no doubt that the emphasis in the resurrection stories is entirely on the mission as being logically prior to all other deeds and results of the Spirit.

THE THEOLOGICAL NEGLECT OF THE MISSION

In view of these facts, it seems entirely ununderstandable that during many centuries and even today, the mission has hardly played any large role in dogmatical thinking. Though this fact cannot be excused, it can be explained. During many periods of history, there was hardly such a reality as mission; the church controlled the whole of society and what was beyond this Christian culture was almost unknown. That situation changed in the sixteenth century. The Roman Catholic Church began to display an impressive missionary activity. The Protestant churches slowly followed from the seventeenth century. In these centuries the bearers of the missionary enterprise were Christian governments: Spain, Portugal, the Republic of the Netherlands, Great Britain, etc. In the eighteenth century in the Protestant world new initiatives were created by little groups of devout Christians, and in the nineteenth century this was done by missionary societies. Governments had no need of a deeper reflection on the theological place of the mission, and groups and societies had no time for it. The official church, and even more its theological faculties generally lived a long distance from these activities and problems. In the second half of the nineteenth century, the mission groups tried to fill their own need for theological reflection. (We think, e.g., of the works of Gustav Warneck.) However, this did not bridge the gulf which existed between mission and ecclesiastical theology. Things improved slowly, but only insofar as mission received attention in terms of practical theology, not systematic theology. A real new phase began through the Second World War and the foundation of the World Council of Churches. The enormous extent of secularism was discovered and came into the limelight of theology, together with the renaissance of the other great world religions. We began to understand that the mission belongs to the very essence of the church and that a theology which would speak about God's revelation, apart from the fact that this revelation is a movement of sendings, would not speak about the biblical revelation. Men like Walter Freytag, Hendrik Kraemer, John Mackay, to mention only a few, have given much effort toward building a bridge between the insights of the mission and official theology.

Up until now we cannot say, however, that these efforts have succeeded according to the high importance of the matter involved. A number of good monographs on this subject have been published, but in the main dogmatical handbooks which appeared in Europe in the last decades, the mission is either entirely neglected or only touched on in passing, that is, in connection with the catholicity of the church. There is one great exception, however: Barth's *Church Dogmatics* IV, 3. In IV, 1, Barth treats the content of faith under the aspect of God's condescendence; in IV, 2, he treats it under the aspect of the result of God's condescendence, i.e., the exaltation of man; in IV, 3, he treats it under the prophetical aspect of the truth which has to be proclaimed in the world. So this last volume deals with Christ's prophetic office, sin as lie, the calling of man, the mission of the church, and the Christian hope. The highly original and fruitful composition of Volume IV in general, and the way in which Barth treats the whole of theology under the missionary aspect in IV, 3, have not yet found the attention which they deserve. Therefore, I regret to say that the highly necessary enrichment of systematic theology by taking in the mission as an essential element in God's mighty deeds is still ahead of us.

The bad consequences of this are most keenly felt in the doctrine of the Holy Spirit. In Roman Catholic theology, the Spirit is mainly the soul and sustainer of the church. In Protestant theology he is mainly the awakener of individual spiritual life in justification and sanctification. So the Spirit is either institutionalized or individualized. And both of these opposite approaches are conceived in a common pattern of an introverted and static pneumatology. The Spirit in this way is the builder of the church and the edifier of the faithful, but not the great mover and driving power on the way from the One to the many, from Christ to the world. In one of the very rare theological works on the relation between the Spirit and mission, the American missionary Harry R. Boer writes: "Much has been written about the work of the Holy Spirit in the salvation of men, but very little about his crucial significance for the missionary witness of the Church."[1] This situation is probably to the detriment of the mission, but surely to the detriment of theology, which suffers a great impoverishment indeed in that it is oriented to situations far more than to movements. In neglecting rather than reflecting the great movement of the Spirit, it distorts the whole content of faith and is an accomplice to the individualistic and institutionalistic introversion and egotism still found in the churches of today.

<h2>THE CHRISTOLOGICAL-ESCHATOLOGICAL CONTEXT</h2>

Mission is far more than a minor practical instrument in the work of salvation. It is directly linked up, on the one hand, with the person and work of Jesus Christ and, on the other hand, with the great future. The first connection is particularly evident in Jesus' title "Servant of the Lord." The question of whether the mysterious Servant in Second Isaiah is meant to be the great missionary to the Gentiles or the one through whom God's salvation of Israel will become known throughout the earth is still disputed. At any rate it is clear that the work of the Servant demands the whole world as his stage and sounding board. God has put his Spirit upon him with the ultimate goal that he may bring forth to the nations the justice of the Lord, his *mishpat*, his revolutionary and merciful covenant-order (Isa. 42:1). That Jesus himself had no missionary aims is not contrary to this fact. He came to be revealed to and to be acknowledged by the elected people, in order that through him this people might attain the goal of its election: to be God's light to the nations. Jesus as the Servant of the Lord is the representative of Israel as Israel is God's priestly representative toward the nations. The New Testament Christology is based on the conception of representation and therefore immediately implies a movement by which the blessings of the One go to the many for which they are meant.

When this movement has come to an end, God's aim is attained and the great future is fulfilled. Therefore the missionary movement stands also in an eschatological context, which is no other context than the christological one, for Christ is the inaugurator and the first fruits of the eschaton. With the descent of his Spirit, the last days have dawned, and they will not be finished until the gospel of the Kingdom is preached throughout the whole world as a testimony to all nations (Matt. 24:14). The meaning of these last days is that the Spirit is poured out on all flesh and that the saving presence of the Lord will be acknowledged by people of all languages, races, classes, and ages (Acts 2). That is what the Spirit does. He forms the unity of the christological and the eschatological pole of God's saving work. He is the expansion of the divine saving presence over the earth. He is the way from the One to the many, from the middle to the end of the times, from the center to the ends of the earth.

One consequence of all this is that we no longer can conceive of the mission as a mere instrument in Christ's saving work, as the way by which the mighty acts of incarnation, atonement, and resurrection are transmitted to the next generation and the remoter nations. Of course, all that is also true. But as the transmission of the mighty acts, the mission is itself a mighty act as well as atonement and resurrection. All these other acts would never be known as mighty acts of God without this last one: the movement of the missionary Spirit. This last mighty act is the gate through which we enter all the preceding acts. This last act still goes on. Of its ongoing accomplishment we are witnesses.

THE SPIRIT'S EXECUTION OF THE MISSIONARY TASK

From what has just been said, it follows that we cannot say that the other mighty acts are God's deeds and that the missionary work is merely the human response to these deeds as an activity of men. In all God's deeds, he is the author and the inspirer; and in them all, men are involved as willing or unwilling instruments. So the Spirit of Christ is the divine subject of mission. He, not we, will convince the world (John 16:8). In John 15:26-27, Jesus says: "... the Spirit of truth ... will bear witness to me; and you also are witnesses ..." That is no synergism in the ordinary sense of the word. Man is active and responsible. In everything, however, he is —to his comfort and humiliation—an instrument of the Spirit. Therefore, "do not be anxious how you are to speak or what you are to say . . . for it is not you who speak, but the Spirit of your Father speaking through you" (Matt. 10:19-20).

Spirit and speaking therefore belong together. This connection is far more dominant than we are inclined to believe. Most of us, consciously or unconsciously, are still deeply influenced by what I am almost inclined to call "the myth of the inner, individual, spiritual life." The New Testament does not know this myth. In general the Bible is less pious than we are: With striking frequency we are told that the main fruit of the Spirit is that he opens our mouths and encourages us to speak. In Acts we repeatedly read that when the Holy Spirit fell on men they began to prophesy and to speak in tongues (2:4; 10:46; 19:6). Paul considers prophecy the main gift of the Spirit (1 Cor. 14:1), more important than speaking in tongues, because "he who prophesies speaks to men for their upbuilding and encouragement and consolation" (14:3). The Spirit, in bestowing his gifts upon men, is from the beginning aiming at their equipment for the great work of transmission.

All this means that the Spirit's main instrument in his great movement is the word as the servant of the Word. So the reflection on the execution of the missionary task by the Spirit inevitably leads us to the classical problem of the relation between Word and Spirit, a theme which always is treated in the context either of the ecclesiastical means of grace or of personal application, but which has its primary and main place in the context of mission.

THE SPIRIT AND THE WORD

The work of transmission is implemented by words which mean to be instrumental to the Word of Jesus Christ, the Word of Scripture. That Word is never a mere human word; in it the Spirit himself is present. The Word is his instrument. Since the Reformation discovered this "sacramental" meaning of the word of preaching, "in, with, and under" which the Spirit of Christ is really present, much thinking has been done on understanding the relation between Word and Spirit. Originally there was no difference on this point between Lutherans and Reformed. However, when the difficulties involved came to the minds of the theologians, the two groups were inclined to give different answers. The Lutherans were mainly concerned with emphasizing the real and active presence of the Spirit in the preached Word, with the result that where the Word is the Spirit also is. They could rightly appeal to different biblical texts,[2] e.g., "so shall my word . . . not return to me empty, but it shall accomplish that which I purpose" (Isa. 55:11). They could also think of the fact that in the Old Testament the word (*dabar*) is never a sheer word, but a decision and a power, and so a parallel of the word *ruach* (cf. Ps. 33:6). Thus the Lutherans preferred to describe the working of the Spirit as occurring "through the Word," *per verbum*.

Consequently, the Word is never without a spiritual influence. Nevertheless, the Word in many cases does not create faith. How can that be explained? Later generations of Lutherans ascribed that lack of result to a certain degree of free will in man, by which he can resist the Spirit. This explanation was unacceptable to the Reformed theologians, and moreover it was in contrast with the Lutheran Augsburg Confession, which declares that the Holy Spirit works faith through the Word "where and when it pleases God" (*ubi et quando visum est Deo*, Article 5). The Reformers were afraid of synergism and of a kind of word-magic on the Lutheran side. They preferred to describe the working of the Spirit as occurring "together with the Word," *cum verbo*. They did not dare to say that where the Word is the Spirit is also. The Spirit can work outside of the Word and the preached word can remain without effect. If it has effect, it is because of an additional working of the Spirit. They also could appeal to a series of biblical words,[3] e.g., the words in Acts 16:14 about Lydia: "The Lord opened her heart to give heed to what was said by Paul." The dangerous consequences of this position were bound to come, however. If the opening of the heart does not come through the Word itself, but must be expected from another action of the Spirit alongside the Word, the hearers are inclined to give little heed to the Word and

to wait for the inner signs of the opening of the heart. This inclination inaugurated the Reformed Pietism of the sixteenth and
seventeenth centuries which is characterized by a basic introversion and, accordingly, by a lack of certainty of faith.

As so often in the unprofitable debates between Lutherans and
Reformed, there was truth and untruth on both sides. There was
truth in the basic assumptions, untruth in many of the consequences and even more in the polemical negations. To begin with
the Lutherans: They truly said that the Spirit is present and active
in the Word; they wrongly tried to maintain this position by a
kind of synergism, in which the initiative passes from the Spirit
to the hearer. The Reformed assumption—that the Word can remain empty—is an equally bad solution; though we cannot avoid
speaking, as the Reformed fathers did, of the necessity of an additional working of the Spirit. We are not allowed, however, to separate this working from the Spirit-power in the Word itself. On the
contrary, if the Lord opens the heart, he does it in such a way that
we give heed to the Word. The testimony of the Spirit in our hearts
is not heard in our hearts but in the recognition of the testimony of
the Spirit in the Word. The Spirit moves through the world in the
shape of the Word in its various forms. The Word is the instrument of the Spirit. But the Spirit is not the prisoner of the Word,
nor does the Word work automatically. The Word brings the Spirit
to the heart, and the Spirit brings the Word within the heart.

SPIRIT, MISSION, CHURCH

If we discover the fundamental place of the Spirit's missionary
activity, we can longer be content with the traditional way in which
the relation between mission and church is posed. The mission is
more than a practical, necessary instrument in the expansion of the
church. The mission is not at the disposal of the church; both
are at the disposal of the Spirit. This conviction leads to the
question of whether we should not convert the thesis and say
that the church is not more than the instrument, or an instrument,
in the great mission of the Spirit. Can the church ever consider

itself as an end in itself? Is that not ecclesiastical narcissism? The great danger of the church all over the world is indeed the danger of introversion. As soon as that is her attitude, she shirks her calling to participate in the great movement from the One to the universe; she becomes static and, as such, disobedient. "You are . . . God's own people, that you may declare the wonderful deeds of him who called you out of darkness into his marvelous light" (1 Peter 2:9).

Nevertheless, we do not solve the problem by converting a wrong thesis. In saying that the church is the instrument of the mission, we speak a half-truth. The relation between the two has more aspects. The church is at the same time the provisional result of the mission. The movement of the Spirit has an end—it is not an end in itself. That end is beyond the church; it is that "the earth shall be full of the knowledge of the LORD as the waters cover the sea" (Isa. 11:9). Insofar, the church cannot be an end in itself; it is the instrument of the ongoing movement. But as a provisional result, the church is a kind of result in which the movement came to its end. Insofar, it is a little bit of realized Kingdom, a prophecy of the *symmorphia* to which the Spirit is pressing forward. We can therefore speak of the double aspect of the church: realization of the Kingdom and instrument of the Kingdom. Both aspects lose their character as soon as they isolate themselves from one another. A static and introverted church, which refuses to be a servant, is for that reason no longer a realization of the Kingdom; however impressive her doctrine, liturgy, and organization may be, she has lost the heart of the matter. A church which would be a mere dynamic, extroverted, activistic movement would not be the divine instrument, because it would not preach by its own existence; it would have no winning force; it would offer no home. The strongest missionary force of the church is always "in demonstration of the Spirit and power" (1 Cor. 2:4).

SPIRIT, MISSION, PERSONAL SALVATION

As a parallel to the previous problem, we must finally say some words about the relation between personal salvation and witness as ends of the Spirit in the individual Christian life. During almost the whole of church history, personal salvation has been considered the main goal of the Spirit. For innumerable Christians that is still the case. They consider participation in the missionary movement as being a job for official missionaries or for higher-level Christians, but not as an essential element of all Christian life. In recent years, we are beginning to discover how heretical this static image of Christian life is. It is even more than static—it is egotistical; Christians are so busy with their eternal salvation and their private edification that they have no time left for their neighbor who has not yet been reached by the movement of the Spirit. The sharpest criticism against this attitude is found in Barth's Volume IV, 3, which I mentioned before. He points to the fact that the Bible contains only stories of calling, not stories of conversion as such. If personal salvation becomes the goal of Christian life, then Christ would be only a means to that end, and the Christian would become a mere consumer. Let me quote only one strong passage: "Can the community of Jesus Christ . . . really be only, or at any rate essentially and decisively, a kind of institute of salvation, the foremost and comprehensive *medium salutis,* as Calvin self-evidently assumed and said? Is not every form of egocentricity excused and even confirmed and sanctified, if egocentricity in this sacred form is the divinely willed meaning of Christian existence and the Christian song of praise consists finally only in a many-tongued but monotonous *pro me, pro me,* and similar possessive expressions?"[4] After what has been said before in this chapter, it is unnecessary to show how salutary words like these are. We can understand that for Barth the goal of Christian life is not personal salvation but being a witness. We may rightly say with him that only in the active participation in the movement of the Spirit can the certainty of personal salvation come into being and be tested. I wonder, however, whether Barth is not in danger of expelling one one-sidedness by introducing another. Here also we must say: The movement of the Spirit has an end; it is not an end in itself. We witness to that which we have received in order that the other may also receive it. What we have received is the communion with God, through Jesus Christ, that is our salvation. At the same time communion means communication, participation in the blessings and in the tasks of the Kingdom. In that Kingdom we are neither mere consumers nor mere laborers. We consume in order to work, and we work in order that others may consume. Here, as well as in the relation between mission and church, one aspect cannot be subordinated to the other. To our thinking they are interrelated so closely that we understand the unity of these aspects only in the great reality of the Kingdom which moves in the Spirit from the sacrificed and risen Lord to its ultimate goal in the community of the saved.

III

THE SPIRIT AND THE CHURCH

In this chapter we must consider the question, Does the relation of the Spirit to the church precede that to the individual or the other way round? If mission is the basic preceding activity, what, then, is the next step? Is it the converting and sanctifying work of the Spirit in the heart of the individual believer? Or is it the up-building of the church with Word and sacrament, ministry and community? The answer to this question has a far-reaching influence, as history shows. It is not a mere theological answer; it decides the shape of our Christian faith.

In the ancient creeds there is no doubt about the order: "I believe in the Holy Ghost; the Holy Catholic Church; the communion of Saints; the forgiveness of sins." We can assume that in these articles the Spirit is conceived of as giving and controlling what is mentioned after him: church, community, forgiveness. All these are fruits of the Spirit. And the collective fruits come first, after that the blessing of the individual with the forgiveness of his sins. In this order the church is meant as the primary manifestation and instrument of the spiritual presence of the risen Lord. In a famous Whitsun sermon on the Holy Spirit and the church, Augustine said: "What the soul is for the body of a man, that is the Holy Spirit for the body of Christ, which is the Church; what the soul works in all the members of the one body, that the Spirit works in the whole of the Church." He even extends this metaphor and reminds his hearers of the fact that an amputated member misses the soul, the *anima*, the life. "So a Christian is a catholic as long as he lives in the body; when he has been cut off and has become a heretic, the Spirit does not follow such an amputated member."[1] The words of the great church father had an age-long influence and are particularly characteristic of the way in which the Roman Catholic Church felt and feels about the working of the Spirit toward the community and toward the individual. The Spirit is the soul of the church. That is his primary relation. And the individual partakes of the Spirit to the extent in which he partakes of the sacramental and hierarchical life of the church. We can understand that this way of solving the question would sooner or later lead to a distortion and impoverishment of the relation between the Lord and the individual believer. For the individual the Spirit is hidden in the totality of the ecclesiastical functions and is even another name for these. In Denzinger's *Enchiridion Symbolorum* we find only a few pronouncements about the work of the Spirit here and now, while almost all concern the relation of the Spirit to the different sacraments.[2] This poor and one-sided result explains why many devout Catholics make the impression on Protestants that they have no personal relation to the Lord: because that relation is swallowed up by their relation to the ecclesiastical institution.

We would not be fair, however, if we let it go at that. Denzinger does not quote the remarkable encyclical of Pope Leo XIII of 1897, called *Divinum Illud Munus*. This document also emphasizes the activity of the Spirit in the hierarchical structure. "For by him the bishops are instituted," as well as the priests, with the authority to forgive sins. In that connection Leo quotes emphatically the words of Augustine about the Spirit as the soul of the church. The new element is that Leo distinguishes between an activity of the Spirit in the church and in baptized individuals. Though this last activity is founded on the sacraments of baptism and confirmation, it is described in lofty phraseology as work of illumination, renewal, and regeneration. This is in spite of the curious words with which the pope introduces this section, saying that this work of the Spirit "is not less admirable [than his work in the church], though it is a little more difficult to understand, also because it is hidden from all view of the eyes."[3] One may wonder whether the work of the Spirit in the church is more manifest than in the individual. If this is a real problem at all, one can argue in both directions. The encyclical does not speak about the relation between the two works of the Spirit.

Another important document from this point of view is the encyclical *Mystici Corporis* issued by Pope Pius XII in 1943. This letter also pays much attention to the work of the Holy Spirit. In some sense, however, it is of lesser importance than Leo's encyclical. Pius XII was troubled about the increasing influence of the so-called *nouvelle théologie* which, in his opinion, stressed the spiritual side of the church to the detriment of its hierarchical structure. He agrees with this group in emphasizing the work of the Spirit in the church and in its members, but he reminds them constantly of the fact that the Spirit's primary work is the creation and preservation of the sacramental and hierarchical structure and that the individual is fully dependent on that structure for his participation in the work of the Spirit. The Spirit, "who though present in all the members and working in them in a divine way, works in the inferior members through the ministry of the superior ones." "For as the divine redeemer sent the Paraclete, the Spirit of truth, who as his representative had to take the hidden guidance of the Church upon himself, so he instructed Peter and his successors that they would make him manifest on earth by their government of the Christian community."[4] Here we read that the Spirit as the hidden ruler and the papacy as the visible ruler of the church are the two means by which Christ is acting in his church. In view of this and innumerable other more or less official statements, we are entitled to say that in Roman Catholic theology the Spirit is mainly the creator of the church as a sacramental and institutional reality. The connection between the Spirit and the individual is mainly indirect. It takes place insofar as the individual partakes of the institute of which the Spirit is the soul. However, even in connection with the church the Spirit is not often mentioned. The reason probably is that the application of the work of Christ to the later generations is mainly ascribed to the Virgin Mary. The encyclical *Mystici Corporis* ends with a panegyric to her, presenting her as the one who, by her intercession, obtained the descent of the Spirit and who now fosters the mystical body of Christ as she once fostered the baby Jesus. The Protestant objection—that Mary replaces Christ—is not quite right. Mary is far more the visible representative of the Spirit, the one who mediates between Christ and us and applies his benefits to us.

As a final remark we must add, however, that the deep and quick renewal in the Catholic Church in the last years, affecting so many age-old convictions, has not left this position untouched. A striking example is the book of Father Henry on *l'Esprit-Saint* which reverses the traditional order completely; it pays the fullest attention to the insights of biblical theology and in connection with it to the work of the Spirit in the individual soul, whereas the relation of the Spirit to the church plays only a minor role.[5] It is yet too early to say what this and other symptoms will mean for the change in the trend of Roman Catholic theology.

After what has just been said, it is entirely understandable that the Reformation sought new ways of interpreting the triangular relation Spirit-church-individual. All the Reformers experienced and formulated a new direct relation between the Spirit and the individual. One can even say that the Reformation was born out of this experience, and that it was clear to its followers that the Roman Catholic Church had no place for this experience. That does not mean that all Reformation churches and groups agreed about the way in which the relation between the Spirit and the individual, on the one hand, and between the Spirit and the church, on the other hand, had to be described and to be brought into mutual connection. In many ways the clearest position was the position of what often is called "radical Protestantism." This type stood directly opposite the Roman Catholic type. Whereas the Catholic type considered the relation between the Spirit and the church as a direct one and that between the Spirit and the individual as an indirect one, based on the first, the radical or "spiritual" form of Protestantism advocated the exact reversal of this order. For it the Spirit is meant for the individual. The heart of the true believer is his dwelling place. Is there any place left for a relation between the Spirit and the church? This question has found differ-

ent answers. We think of the Anabaptists, Kaspar von Schwenck-
feld, the Quakers, Delabadie and his group, or Tersteegen. For
some, the church exists only as the invisible bond between all pious
souls in the world. Others believe in the true church as a group in
the core of the institutional churches. Still others emphasize the
calling of the regenerated to secede from the official churches and
to found the true church of the children of God. And some reject
all kind of visible community because they refuse basically to go
beyond religious individualism. In no case is the church more than
the assembly of those who recognize one another as bearers of the
same Spirit. Their church is at most an organized group or sect, in
many cases a loose convention or conventicle. In every case this
church, as such, is not the work of the Spirit but is a human consequence of the spiritual work in individual hearts, founded on the
natural impulse of congenials to seek out one another. So the relation of the Spirit to this community never can be more than an indirect one. Hence it is quite natural that the group is dissolved or
that secessions take place as soon as the participants no longer
recognize one another as bearers of the same Spirit.

This radical Protestant movement has split into two directions,
the one liberal, the other orthodox. In the liberal tradition the
Spirit became more and more identified with the human mind and
its religious, philosophical, and ethical ideas, as they were conceived
in the period of the Enlightenment and in German Idealism. The
orthodox tradition became the pietistic movement with its later off-
shoots of evangelicalism and fundamentalism; even the Pentecostal
movement can be seen as a late fruit of this large tradition. Here
the natural human spirit is not a part of the divine Spirit but, on
the contrary, the enemy of God's Spirit which has to be converted
and regenerated. In spite of these deep contrasts, however, both
groups stand on a common ground, because they see the Spirit
mainly as the relation between God and the individual soul. The
spiritual and cultural blessing as a consequence of this view cannot
be denied. This wing of Protestantism has greatly contributed to
the personal experience of Christian faith and to the creation of the
"inner-directed man" with his notion of responsibility, particularly
on the American continent. In Europe these groups fulfill a salutary

function in countries with dominant national church institutes, as in Great Britain, Scandinavia, and southern Europe. Their weakness everywhere is that they have no clear idea about the relation between the Spirit and the church and that to most of them the church is hardly more than a human community.

The survey we have given thus far makes us eager to know what position the classical Reformation took in this dilemma. If we inquire into the position of Calvin, the answer at first glance seems to be clear and simple. After having dealt with Christ and his redemptive work in the second book of the *Institutes*, Calvin gives us, as the heading of the third book, the words "The Way in Which We Receive the Grace of Christ: What Benefits Come to Us from It, and What Effects Follow." In this book he deals with the subjects: faith, regeneration, penitence, the life of the Christian, justification, good works, Christian liberty, prayer, and predestination. There is no doubt that the individual believer is in the center as the receiver of these spiritual gifts. The heading of the fourth book reads: "The External Means or Aids by Which God Invites Us into the Society of Christ and Holds Us Therein." These means are: the church, preaching, the sacraments, church discipline, and state government. It seems clear that to Calvin the church is not more than an outward though very important means to the process of the encounter between the Spirit and the individual believer as described in the third book. Therefore, Emil Brunner in his *Dogmatics* concludes: ". . . Calvin regards the Church as an external support of faith . . . it is not essentially bound up with faith but is only a support, though certainly a necessary one, and explicitly an *external* support of faith. Between faith and the Church there is no inner necessary relation but only an accidental, subsidiary one, in which faith is essentially regarded as something individual, the fellowship of faith being added to it as something which does not belong to its nature. That is to say that although Calvin in practical matters was in the highest degree a Church-man and a founder of churches, he makes an individualistic separation of faith from the Church. Believers indeed require the Church, but they are believers even apart from it. That is also the customary conception of reformed Protestantism."[6]

Brunner in his interpretation of Calvin is here in accordance with many scholars on both sides of the ocean. The difference is that many welcome Calvin's individualism, whereas Brunner deplores it.

Personally, I believe that this is a simplification of Calvin's view. Brunner appeals to the title of the fourth book, according to which God through the church "Invites Us into the Society of Christ and Holds Us Therein." Does that mean, as Brunner interprets it, that we are faithful even apart from the church? I myself draw the opposite conclusion: No one can come to the community with Christ, i.e., become faithful, apart from God's working through the church! The title of the first chapter reads: "The True Church with Which as Mother of All the Godly We Must Keep Unity." Calvin explains the word "mother" by saying that the knowledge of the visible church is useful and even necessary to us, because "there is no other way to enter into life unless this mother conceive us in her womb, give us birth, nourish us at her breast, and, lastly, unless she keep us under her care and guidance until, putting off mortal flesh, we become like the angels" (IV, 1, 4). That sounds far from individualistic! In the next paragraph he says: "God breathes faith into us only by the instrument of his gospel, as Paul points out that 'Faith comes from hearing.'" We can multiply these quotations with many others to prove that for Calvin the church, and particularly the ministry of the Word, as a rule is the only means by which the Spirit draws men into the communion with Christ. Nevertheless, the total picture of Calvin's ideas is not quite clear. Brunner does not speak as he does without reason. In the second sentence of the fourth book, Calvin writes: "Since, however, in our ignorance and sloth (to which I add fickleness of disposition) we need outward helps to beget and increase faith within us, and advance it to its goal, God has also added these aids that he may provide for our weakness. And in order that the preaching of the gospel might flourish, he deposited this treasure in the church." These words give the impression that Calvin sees the external organization of the church as a concession of God in view of our poor and sinful nature. The ideal situation would be that the Spirit can meet us through Scripture, without such outward help. Therefore Calvin can first describe this meeting apart from the church.

At any rate, it is clear that Calvin's view cannot be identified with that of radical Protestantism nor with that of Roman Catholicism. With the latter, he emphasizes the necessity of the church for our salvation, but he does not so much think of a sacramental, hierarchical institute as of the ministry of the preaching of the gospel. With the Spiritualists, he emphasizes the fact that the aim of the Spirit is to dwell in the heart of the individual, but he sees the church not only as the human result of this work but also as the divine ground of it.

The Reformed Church is the daughter of the Catholic Church type and the mother of the Free Church type. She has affinities with both. Small wonder that she, in different areas and different periods, leans more toward one or the other. In her confessions and theological handbooks she usually follows Calvin's order: first the Spirit's relation to the individual, after that the relation to the church. Some reverse the order, however, as did John Owen in his *Pneumatologia* (1674), and Abraham Kuyper in *The Work of the Holy Spirit* (1888), and Brunner in the third volume of his *Dogmatics*. Herman Bavinck in his famous *Reformed Dogmatics* follows the traditional order but nevertheless writes: "The individual believer is born out of the womb of the Church. The *ecclesia universalis* precedes the individual *fideles*, as in each organism the whole precedes the parts."[7] A similar duality can be found in Karl Barth also. It is characteristic for the Reformed confession, which wants to maintain both, to give full emphasis to the relation between the Spirit and the individual and, at the same time, to recognize that the church is a creation not of men but of the Spirit. So it is understandable that the order between both remained undecided in the Reformed confession. We believe that we must try to go a step beyond the traditional position and to reach a decision about the order.

In my opinion the right order is: first the church, after that the individual. In the Scriptures the Spirit always begins with individuals who are not individuals but representatives who include a whole community. On the highest level that is true of Jesus Christ himself. In calling his disciples, he makes them enter into the community with him and with one another. So they enter into the church. We read of a similar event in Acts 2. The Spirit is poured out on a community, making it the witnessing church to which the attending individuals are invited. And the Epistles stress the fact that the individuals, like living stones, have to be built into a spiritual house and by their gifts have to contribute to the upbuilding of the body. This does not mean that the work of the Spirit in the individual is subordinated to that in the church. One can as well or even better argue that the proper work of the Spirit is his dwelling in the lives of individuals. This last and highest work presupposes the work in the church, however. And it cannot flourish if the individual is not willing to join the community and contribute to it. As long as we put the individual first, we cannot get the right view on the church as ground and mother of the individual life. If we put the church first, we see how the individual is born out of her, and we are logically led in his direction. The logical order is that Christ points to the mission, the mission points to the church, and the church points to the individual.

THE SPIRIT'S TWOFOLD WORK IN THE CHURCH

In the previous section we were dealing with a question of order, but at the same time with more than that. Those churches and theologians who are inclined to give priority to the church largely think of the church in terms of Word and sacrament, of institution and ministry. We learned that from several Roman Catholic utterances. It would be easy to add many other Roman Catholic, Eastern Orthodox, Anglican, and also Lutheran quotations. Those churches and theologians who are inclined to give priority to the individual mainly think of the church in terms of community, of an assembly of individual believers. This is the main approach in the Free Churches.

Now that we have decided to give priority to the church, this cannot mean that we decide that the nature of the church is formulated in the way in which the Catholic churches used to do. It is typical for our Reformed position that in ecclesiology we want to keep both approaches together and to see the church under an institutional as well as under a community aspect. It would be unfair to say that this intention is absent in other churches. My impression is that, under the influence of biblical theology and the ecumenical movement, we find in all churches and theologies a trend toward emphasizing those aspects in ecclesiology which were neglected before and toward building a fuller and more complementary ecclesiology than former generations did. The most striking example is the newest Roman Catholic theology which prefers to speak of the church not as an institution but as "the people of God" and which emphasizes so greatly the place of the laity in the church. Other good examples of a growing consensus in this field are the excellent study *One Lord One Baptism* of the "Commission on Faith and Order"[8] and the preparatory reports for the Conference on Faith and Order in Montreal. We do not forget that in this context we are not interested in ecclesiology as such, but in the way in which the Spirit works in and through the church. The different positions help us to understand that we should not try to choose a one-sided approach, nor should we bring the work of the Spirit in the church under a single heading. First we seek to discover what the institutional side of the church has to do with the Holy Spirit. Next we want to see how the community element is the work of the Spirit. Finally we have to ask how both these sides are related to one another in the one action of the Spirit.

THE INSTITUTIONAL ASPECT

For many Protestants it is difficult to understand that the Spirit has anything to do with the institutional and organizational character of the church. The reason is that they have such an individualistic and spiritualistic or, at best, personalistic conception of the Spirit that they do not understand that God created structures as well as persons and that in his saving work he is also interested in structures insofar as they can serve his purposes. The New Testament has not the slightest trouble in seeing that the Spirit is connected with outward acts, ministries, and organizations. I shall mention seven of these connections.

First, the Spirit is related to baptism: "For by one Spirit we were

all baptized into one body" (1 Cor. 12:13). "But you were washed
. . . in the name of the Lord Jesus Christ and in the Spirit of our
God" (1 Cor. 6:11). (Cf. Acts 2:38; Col. 2:12; Eph. 4:5; 5:26;
probably also Titus 3:5-6.)

Second, the laying on of hands is an instrument used to transmit
the Holy Spirit. "Then they laid their hands on them and they received the Holy Spirit" (Acts 8:17). "Hence I remind you to re-
kindle the gift of God that is within you through the laying on of
my hands" (2 Tim. 1:6). (Cf. Acts 19:6.)

Third, the Spirit has to do with Holy Communion. "For . . . we
were all . . . made to drink of one Spirit" (1 Cor. 12:13). This must
be because the Spirit is the risen Christ himself acting in his congregation and Communion is the institution of the same Christ
for his continuous re-presentation.

Fourth, the Holy Spirit has to do with the proclamation of
the gospel as his creation and instrument. For he who supplies the
Spirit to us does that by hearing with faith (Gal. 3:5), because the
Word of God is the sword of the Spirit (Eph. 6:17). (Cf. 2 Cor.
3:8; 1 Thess. 1:5; 1 Peter 1:12.)

Fifth, the Spirit has to do with authority and discipline in the
church. Jesus breathed on his Apostles and said: "Receive the Holy
Spirit. If you forgive the sins of any, they are forgiven; if you retain
the sins of any, they are retained" (John 20:22-23).

Sixth, the ministry of the Apostles in general is closely related to
the work of the Spirit. The Second Letter to the Corinthians
strongly testifies to that relation. We think also of the words of the
apostolic assembly in Acts 15:28: "For it has seemed good to the
Holy Spirit and to us . . ."

Finally, the Spirit uses the ministry in general as his instrument.
That is the presupposition of the description of the ministry in the
Pastoral Letters. It is the risen Christ, that is, the Spirit, who gave
gifts to men. "And his gifts were that some should be apostles,
some prophets, some evangelists, some pastors and teachers . . .
for building up the body of Christ" (Eph. 4:11-12). Therefore, in
Acts 20:28, Paul can say to the elders of Ephesus: "Take heed to
yourselves and to all the flock, in which the Holy Spirit has made
you guardians . . ."

In Protestant theology there is a remarkable apprehension about acknowledging fully the validity and relevance of this work of the Spirit. There is a steady anxiety that a profound attention to these aspects might lead to a conception in which the Spirit becomes the prisoner of the church instead of the church's being the instrument of the Spirit. This anxiety is quite understandable. The Reformation was, in part, a protest against a church which behaved as if she had the Spirit in store; and until today, in many countries and in many circumstances, the Roman Catholic Church still makes the impression of being a big depot of the Spirit who is distributed in the form of sacraments. As the Reformation theology cannot deny the close connection between the Spirit on the one hand and preaching, sacraments, ministry, and organization on the other hand, the difference with the Roman Catholic position is often sought in the emphasis on the sovereignty of the Spirit over against his means. It is a typical Reformed position to point to the freedom of the Spirit who can use all these means but who can also refuse to do so and work outside of them. His coming to us is an act of free grace. We do not dispose of it. We can pray for it. As the famous Dutch theologian Noordmans expressed it characteristically: "We cannot say (it may be said respectfully) that when we go to church, God goes to church also."[9] The defenders of this position point particularly to several passages in the Old Testament: to the stories of God who abandons his Ark (1 Sam. 4) and his temple (Ezek. 10) and to Jeremiah's address at the gate of the temple in which he said: "Do not trust in these deceptive words: 'This is the temple of the LORD, the temple of the LORD, the temple of the LORD' " (7:4). In the New Testament they point to 1 Corinthians 10 where Paul says that although the fathers were all baptized in Moses and all ate and drank the same supernatural food, nevertheless, God was not pleased with most of them.

That is all true and these prophetic words are often overheard in our institutionalized Christendom. We are in danger, however, of drawing the wrong conclusion from these facts. Nowhere is it suggested that we cannot trust God's presence in these means. That presence is undisputed. It is exactly that divine presence which is overlooked by the people. They put their confidence in the

temple instead of in the God whom they meet in the temple. They
avoid the real encounter and the consequent obedience. They prefer a magical relation which offers security without obedience. God
remained really present in the Ark and in the supernatural food,
but it was no longer a presence of grace but of wrath. What was
meant as a blessing turned into an accusation. God's promises do
not fail. We cannot play off his sovereignty against his promises.
"This is my body," "This is my blood," "Where two or three are
gathered in my name, there I am in the midst of them," "I am with
you always"—all these promises are valid. We can meet the living
Lord in his Spirit through the means which he has given. The decisive question is whether we really want to meet him and, as a
consequence of it, whether his real presence in the institutions of
his church will bless us or accuse us. Not his sovereignty, but our
unbelief and disobedience make a separation between God and us.
Therefore, we would do better to reverse the words of Noordmans
which I just quoted, and say: "We cannot say that when God goes
to church, we go to church also." We can never emphasize enough
that the institution and its means are not an end in themselves but
are meant to accomplish the encounter between God and his
people.

The difference between the position of the Roman Catholic
Church and the Reformation can therefore not be sought in a
tighter or looser connection between the Spirit and the institute of
the church. The real difference lies in the priority of the means and
the character of the encounter which is achieved by them. In the
Roman Catholic Church, priority is given to the sacraments over
against the preaching of the Word. This priority is to the detriment
of the personal encounter. It is connected with a more *dingliche*
conception of grace, which is less protected against a transposition
of means and end and therefore sooner subject to prophetic criticism. The Reformation cannot prevent this deviation by making
the real presence of the Spirit in the means doubtful; it can only
be prevented by emphasizing that they are merely the means of the
living Spirit. On this point there is also hope that the cleavage in
the Western church has become smaller in the last years, since so
many Roman Catholic theologians want to reformulate their faith
in personalistic categories.

It will be the duty of Protestant theology to lay off its hydrophobia in connection with the work of the Spirit in the institutional side of the church. Every minister and every member should be fully alive to the fact that in the church we have not to do with human ideas, ceremonies, and activities, but with the authority and the action of the living Spirit, to which all our activities have to be subjected. The discovery of the church as the holy ground on which we are standing, as the great sacrament of God's active presence, in spite of what the Reformers themselves have said, lies still ahead of much so-called Protestantism.

THE COMMUNITY ASPECT OF THE CHURCH

The Holy Spirit is not only working in the church as an institution. He is also the builder of the church as a body, as a communion. We are not only children of our mother the church—we are the church ourselves. Here we must make a sharp distinction, lest we create confusion. We do not speak here about the work of the Spirit in individual hearts, nor even about the gifts which the Spirit bestows on the individual to contribute to the building up of the body. We must limit our concern to the great fact that the church as an institution does not give birth to mere individuals, but creates a real community. Of course this is a communion first with God and then also with the members of the body. Here we are more concerned with the second than with the first, because the communion with God can, if need be, be understood in an individualistic way, as it has been done for centuries, whereas the communion with one another through the communion with the Lord is the typical church-building aspect of the community which the Spirit creates. In the old national churches this great fact was almost forgotten until very recently. If we are more aware of it at the present, it is also because on the American continent the community aspect of the church is so impressively developed.

The church as a community is not the result of the natural impulses of congenial men to seek one another (though this impulse is used in the work of God); it is "a letter from Christ . . . written not with ink but with the Spirit of the living God" (2 Cor. 3:3).

As in our traditional conception Spirit and individual belong closely together, so in Paul the words "Spirit" and "body" are complementary: "There is one body and one Spirit" (Eph. 4:4).

The first evidence of the community-creating action of the Spirit is the fact that in the church the two so bitterly opposed groups, the Jews and the Gentiles, come together to build one body. "For he is our peace, who has made us both one, and has broken down the dividing wall of hostility . . . in whom you also are built into it for a dwelling place of God in the Spirit" (Eph. 2:14, 22). This coming together of the Jews and the Gentiles under the reconciling pressure of the Spirit is exemplary for the way in which the Spirit in the body of Christ overcomes all barriers of national, social, sexual, and racial kind. This body which transcends all natural affinities and all natural diversities stands in the world as the great sign of the unifying power of the Spirit and, as such, as the prophecy of the great future, of the way of living which God has meant for mankind, as the beginning fulfillment of the goal of humanity, of the liberty, equality, and fraternity of the Kingdom.

The *magna charta* of this community is 1 Corinthians 12-14. At first it seems that Paul is mainly interested in the different gifts which the individuals in the congregation of Corinth possess. Paul sees how these gifts, on the one hand, and the lack of sensational gifts, on the other hand, are in danger of separating the body into two groups—one with an inferiority complex, the other with a superiority complex. He points out that the gifts are of no use at all as long as their results are dividing instead of uniting. There-fore, he shows to them a more excellent way (12:31) by emphasiz-ing love, i.e., the love of Christ as the Head and of the members of the body as the center of Christian life, without which the owner of even the highest gifts is but a noisy gong (13). His conclusion is: "Make love your aim, and earnestly desire the spiritual gifts" (14:1) for gifts have meaning only in the context of love and as instruments of love toward the less gifted brethren. So Paul can compare the church with a body in which the diversity is not to the detriment of the unity, but is its necessary supposition and comple-ment. Unity is inconsistent with uniformity. "If all were a single organ, where would the body be?" (12:19). Everyone is dedicated to the service of others and to the service of the whole. Paul even says: ". . . the parts of the body which seem to be weaker are indispensable, and those part of the body which we think less honorable we invest with the greater honor, and our unpresentable parts are treated with greater modesty, which our more presentable parts do not require" (12:22-24). If I understand these words, Paul wants to say that the more gifted members have to honor their less gifted brethren by putting their own gifts into the service of these less honorable members. We have nothing for ourselves. All we have is subjected to the goal "that there may be no discord in the body, but that the members may have the same care for one another" (12:25).

Probably we are inclined to say that this ideal picture of the congregation is far removed from reality. Paul himself would not use this terminology. He would say that, insofar as this is not a reality in our churches, the reason is that we in our disobedience prevent the really present Spirit from doing his work among us.

For a stronger emphasis on and a deeper understanding of this community aspect, it is important to study the problems around the word *koinōnia* in the New Testament. First we think of the words which conclude the Second Letter to the Corinthians: "The grace of the Lord Jesus Christ and the love of God and the fellowship of the Holy Spirit be with you all" (13:14). What do the words *hè koinōnia tou hagiou pneumatos* mean? The grace of the Lord Jesus Christ is the grace which he grants. The love of God is the love which God bestows upon us. It is therefore obvious that we must describe the fellowship of the Spirit as that fellowship or community with God and with one another which is the gift of the Spirit. However, in other cases the genitive after *koinōnia* is a genitive of the object and points to that with which one has fellowship, that in which one partakes. Then the correct translation would be: the participation in the Holy Spirit. The arguments for either translation are equal. In the description of the primitive church in Acts (2:42), we read that "they devoted themselves to the apostles' teaching and fellowship, to the breaking of bread and the prayers." Here the word *koinōnia* stands without any genitive of definition, as a kind of technical term the content of which was well known to the readers. Here also one can argue in both directions. One can think of the fact mentioned two verses later: "And all who believed were together and had all things in common" or of the words: "Now the company of those who believed were of one heart and soul" (4:32). A counterargument is that this community was not yet mentioned when the word koinōnia was used. Therefore, others think of the participation in the gift of the Holy Spirit because, in Acts 2:38, Peter says: ". . . you shall receive the gift of the Holy Spirit." A profound study of these questions has been made by the well-known Anglican theologian L. S. Thornton in his book *The Common Life in the Body of Christ*, who concludes that the emphasis is on the meaning of "participation in"; but he adds: "It must not be adopted, however, in a sense which excludes the other alternative." "The koinonia is ultimately one reality with many aspects." Thornton's definition is: ". . . a relation between individuals which involves common and mutual interest and participation in a common object."[10] I believe that Thornton is right. As so often in the New Testament terminology, there is no either-or. The ambiguity is a sign of multidimensionality. In Philippians 2 we have the same thing. Paul says to his readers: "if there is any koinōnia of the Spirit" which can mean: "if there is any participation in the Spirit" (R.S.V.) or "any sharing of the Spirit" (N.E.B.), but in view of the disunity in the congregation which Paul wants to check, one may also translate: "if the Spirit has created a real fellowship."[11] It is in this last line that the word koinōnia simply means a deed of support as an expression of the community, a service in money or in another way. So Macedonia and Greece have made some koinōnia for the poor fellow Christians in Jerusalem (Rom. 15:26); the Macedonians begged Paul for the favor of the koinōnia in the diaconia toward the saints (2 Cor. 8:4). The author of Hebrews admonishes his readers to do good and "not to forget the koinōnia, for such sacrifices are pleasing to God" (13:16).

We see how the word koinōnia covers two realities, the communication of the Spirit and the communion with one another. Both belong inseparably together. As soon as we come to participate in the reality of the Holy Spirit through Word and sacraments, we enter also by the very same act into community with all those who have the same participation in the Spirit. This two-sided fact excludes two possibilities: It is impossible to have communication with the Holy Spirit in an individualistic way without communion with one another. It is equally impossible to call a community a Christian fellowship as long as the conscious or unconscious bond is rooted in participation in the same national origin, social class, race. The community which the Spirit creates is one of which he himself is the center, in which men recognize one another and are in fellowship with one another for the only reason that they share in the same confession of sin, in the same adoption as children of God, in the same expectancy of the Kingdom, and in the same calling to love and obedience.

THE RELATION BETWEEN THE TWO

The church as a creation of the Spirit is both an institution and a community. This duality poses a big problem to our thinking. We cannot bring these two viewpoints under one heading. They have to be described in different categories. Institutions belong to the world of structures, of objectivities. Communities belong to the world of existence and personalism. Philosophy has struggled during the centuries to see both realities under one heading, but often did so at the cost of one or both or at the cost of their real unity. Theology cannot avoid the problem either. We find it in every realm of God's activity toward us. At the point which we have now reached, the problem is acute, because we have to describe this ecclesiological duality as the work of the one Spirit, and therefore we have to answer the question about the relation of the two aspects.

Often theology acquiesces in just putting both aspects side by side, often adding that their relation is "dialectical" and that they have to be held in tension. We find a deeper and more systematic approach to this problem in the study of the French-Swiss theologian Jean-Louis Leuba, called *Institute and Event. The two ways of God's work according to the New Testament, their difference and their unity* (Neuchâtel, 1950). Though his problem is not entirely identical with ours, ours is also included in the scope of his

study. He shows how everywhere in the work of salvation we find
the togetherness of objective and personal, static and dynamic, con-
tinuous-horizontal and incidental-vertical elements. He even identi-
fies these two trends with the difference between Catholicism and
Protestantism. His conclusion in the field of theology is rather dis-
appointing. Not only does he identify the two tendencies in the
early church with the Jewish Christians and the Gentile Christians,
but his last word is that of a "fundamental ecclesiastical duality,"
of two trends "equally represented in the church" which "she will
not confuse nor separate."[12] This solution cannot satisfy us. Both
aspects are closely related and presuppose one another. Theology not
only says that both exist, but it says also how both are interrelated in
the unity of God's work. As long as we refuse to do this, we leave it
in the freedom of churches and individuals to prefer one or the
other aspect and to continue a one-sidedness and an opposition
which have no legitimate theological sense.

More attention was paid to this problem in the Montreal Conference on Faith and Order (1963). The North American Report
on Christ and the church devoted a paragraph to "The Church as
Event and Institution." (The European report does not have a
counterpart to it.) The paragraph is carefully phrased and points
to many aspects of the question. It speaks of the two aspects as
"inseparably related one to another, interwoven and complementary," but it thinks mainly of them in terms of "a dialectic of freedom and form." One may wonder whether the institutional side of
the church is adequately described in the word "form." At any rate
it is difficult if not impossible to see freedom and form in a synthesis. Therefore, the report says: "Just as the Church is an activity
and a life in which nature and mission are inseparable, and in which
being and act are never to be set in opposition, so also the Church
is inseparably both event and institution. By 'event' we mean here
the dynamic energizing by Christ and the Spirit in the Church,
the spontaneous quality of the human response, and the 'processive'
character of the community's life in grace. By 'institution' we mean
the established relationships and patterns of historical and social
order, stable forms and definite structures." The report has an understandable preference for the event which, as it says, "is the prius

of the Church" of which the institutional elements are both the
result and the vessel. For "event is never without form." The conclusion is: "No easy boundaries, no neat delimitations, no ultimate
disjunctions can be established between the necessary freedom
which marks the Church as 'event' and the necessary ordering
which marks the Church as 'institution.'" The first section in
Montreal also devoted a chapter of its report to this question, under
the title "The Church: Act and Institution." Its pronouncements
are less important than those of the American preparatory report.
It keeps both together and says: "Since God's presence is made
real to us through instituted means, there must be no playing of
charisma and institution against one another."

These statements are not satisfactory insofar as they do not go
beyond the description of the duality and (in the American report)
the description of the close interrelation within this duality. The
reason why these and many other documents remain within the
limits of this duality is, in my opinion, that they see the nature of
the church against a spiritualistic background, i.e., that they see
the Spirit as being without genuine connection with forms and institutions, as an invisible immaterial power which goes from the
heart of God to the heart of the individual. In this way the Spirit
needs also visible forms and actions, but they are strange to his
nature. For that reason duality and eventually close dialectical
interrelation are the last words.

The New Testament which speaks about the Holy Spirit in
such a concrete way does not know this problem of duality. Let me
try to show how some passages and words implicitly contain a solution of our problem.

In Ephesians 4 we hear about the risen Christ, who is identical
with the Spirit and who "gave gifts to men" (vs. 8). These gifts
are, at the beginning of the passage (vs. 7) and at its end (vs. 16),
the charismatic gifts to all members which are necessary for the
upbuilding of the community. Nevertheless there is a certain order
in these gifts. As primary gifts of the risen Christ are mentioned
"that some should be apostles, some prophets, some evangelists,
some pastors and teachers" (vs. 11). Apparently we have to do here
with an institutional element, which is seen as a direct gift of the

Spirit. The Spirit is not only interested in hearts or in faithful communities but also in organizations! However: He is not interested in organizations as ends in themselves, for the passage goes on to say that these gifts were meant "for the equipment of the saints, for the work of the ministry, for building up the body of Christ" (vs. 12) or, as the N.E.B. translates more clearly: "to equip God's people for work in his service, to the building up of the body of Christ." The institute has priority, but it finds its aim in the community to which it is an instrument.

We find a similar structure if we study Paul's use of the word "body," for which I point to the little masterpiece of John A. T. Robinson.[13] For Paul the body can mean: the earthly existence of Christ, the eucharistic body, or the community of the church. Sometimes we see the different meanings shade off into one another (Rom. 7:4; 1 Cor. 10:17). Jesus in his body achieves decisions of eternal importance. These decisions have to be made present in our bodies through baptism (Rom. 6) and through Holy Communion, where his body is present in the eucharistic bread. By this communication with Christ's body we become a communion, the body of Christ in the world. As Augustine said to the partakers in Holy Communion: "You are what you receive."[14] So the work which the Spirit does is a very realistic, bodily work. It is a work of incorporation, implanting us into the crucified and risen *corpus Christi* and so making us to be the *corpus Christi*. And the way of incorporation, the way from the historical to the ecclesiastical body, is the way of being buried with Christ by baptism and being raised out of the water, the way of partaking in his atonement by eating his body and drinking his blood. We see how in the conception of the body the "materialistic" and "spiritualistic," or better, the institutional and community aspects, belong inseparably together. We also see how here, as well as in Ephesians 4, the institutional elements are prior to the community elements, but only because they must found and nourish them.

A parallel trend is shown in Colossians 2 and 3, where the admonition to belong to Christ and to build his community is based on the fact that in Christ the fullness of deity dwells bodily, that he has overcome the elemental powers of the universe by his cross,

that we are circumcized and buried in him by baptism, by which
we ourselves died to those elemental powers and have our lives with
Christ hid in God, so that now in a new freedom we can hold fast
to the Head, from whom the whole body grows according to God's
design.

These examples will suffice to give an insight into the New
Testament unity of sacrament and personal decision, of organization of the ministry and growth of the community, of bodily actions
and spiritual incorporation. Now we must try to find a formulation
for the insights which underlie these and many other Pauline passages.

The movement of the Holy Spirit is the movement of the One
to the many, of the *pars* to the *totum*. The Spirit as Christ in action
does a twofold work: a work of re-presentation, on the one hand,
and of incorporation, on the other. In baptism, preaching, and
eucharist, and in the work of the ministry in general, the Spirit
makes the one Christ present among us. The institute is the way
of his re-presentation. The aim of the re-presentation of Christ with
us is our incorporation into him. We embrace his Word; we die
and rise with him in baptism; we partake of his presence in bread
and wine—and so we are continuously incorporated into his work
once for all. This is the way in which the many become involved
into the life and work of the One. And as the re-presentation finds
its aim in the incorporation, so the incorporation finds its aim in the
building of the community as a prophecy of the new mankind, as
a common being conformed to the image of Christ. We should
therefore not speak of duality, but of a movement, of a chain with
different links. To use another metaphor, we can say: The institutional element and the community element are related to one another as root and fruit. The root is prior to the fruit, but the fruit
is the end as the root is the base. The metaphor is valid also insofar
as the fruit comes and vanishes and the root is the basic and remaining element thanks to which new fruits grow again and again.

We now understand better the tension between the different
church-types which we delineated earlier. The Catholic Church-
type emphasizes the root; the Free Church-type emphasizes the
fruit—both for good reasons and both with the danger that they

underestimate the other element. Perhaps we must say that the underestimation of the fruit is worse than the underestimation of the root. On the other hand, theology as well as practice have taught us that it is easier for institutional churches to acknowledge the significance of the laity and the community than it is for community churches to come to a new appreciation of the institutional structure as a gift of the Spirit. Dr. Hendry in his lectures on the Spirit and the renewal of the church points out that the Spirit works three realities in the church: authority, vitality, and solidarity. Speaking about the problem of authority, he rightly says: "This is the crucial problem in Protestantism, and, it would appear, the most intractable."[15] We shall never come to a full-grown ecclesiology if we do not discover the organic relation between authority and institution on the one hand and community, liberty, and personal decision on the other hand. Here is no either-or. Both elements presuppose one another—the one being the base of the other, the other being the aim of the one.[16] This is the main realm in which a future convergence and unity of Catholic and Protestant theology and church life must be found. It can only be reached if we passionately seek for the higher synthesis into which the partial truths of both sides can be included. As the Spirit is the one who creates and uses both realities, we have to expect our reunion from a deeper understanding of his work and a deeper individual and also ecclesiastical experience of his reality. As Dr. Hendry formulates it, we need "a great act of faith in the Holy Spirit as the author of vitality and solidarity as well as authority."[17]

Finally, we must not forget that we have to see the duality of the church in the wider christological-eschatological context of the Spirit. The beginning and the center of his movement is the work of Jesus Christ, accomplished for us without our help. We have to live by a work which is beyond us, outside of us, a work which has to be presented and re-presented to us. The church as an institute is the way in which this spiritual re-presentation and through which our incorporation takes place. In Word, sacraments, and ministry, Christ is made present to the community of his church. This community in its turn is called to be the means by which Christ is made present to the world. Christ is what the Germans call *das Gegen-*

über (the "over-against") of the church as an institute; the institute is the same with regard to the community; and the community is, likewise, with regard to the world. The institute is not the first root—that is Christ himself. And the community is not the last aim—that is mankind as a whole. So the Spirit draws wider and wider circles around Christ. The church is somewhere in the middle between Christ and the universe, as a partial realization of his goal and as a representative of his deeds and purposes toward the world. The unity of these two aspects is the nature of the church.

IV

THE SPIRIT AND THE INDIVIDUAL

As we saw in the previous chapter, creating and building up the church are the very essence of the Spirit's work. But in God's work the emphasis on the community never leads to collectivism. Not only is this emphasis not to the detriment of the Spirit's relation to the individual, but the collective work of the Spirit is even the necessary supposition of his work in the hearts and the lives of individuals. Jesus Christ is the Head of the body, but at the same time and even for that very reason he is the one who in his pity leaves the ninety-nine and goes after the one who is lost. For as the community comes to its goal only in the individuals, so also do the individuals come to their goal only in the community. Both collectivism and individualism are excluded in the work of the Spirit.

ALTERNATIONS IN HISTORY

This does not alter the fact that in history the church went through periods of distinct collectivism and of distinct individualism. In the Middle Ages the first type was preponderant, in the nineteenth century the second type. Roman Catholicism has a tendency toward the first deviation, Protestantism toward the second. The Reformation was not, as it is often misrepresented, the revolution of the individual against ecclesiastical authority; but it was a deep personalization of the Christian faith—a bringing together of the Word of God and the individual that had never happened before and can never be undone. In the period from the middle of the sixteenth century to the middle of the eighteenth century, the relation between the Spirit and the individual was very much at the core of Protestant thinking. The period produced a rich harvest of theological and devotional literature on this theme, unparalleled in either former or later times. Even a creedal statement was formulated. We think of the so-called Canons of Dort (1619), in which the Reformed Church of the Netherlands, assisted by representatives of several other Reformed churches, not only decided against the Arminians in matters of predestination, but also in the famous chapter III/IV on corruption and conversion gave a description of the work of the Spirit in the human heart, which exercised its influence in the Reformed tradition for a very long time. In many aspects this statement about regenerating grace still holds good today. However, this confession also contains symptoms of a faulty development toward individualism. The biblical context in which the individual has to function plays only a minor role in the canons. The election of Israel in the covenant, Christ as the Elected One, the visible church, the calling of the faithful to witness and service in the world, and the eschatological Kingdom—these wider perspectives of the encounter between the Spirit and the individual are almost neglected, with the consequence that the work of the Spirit is conceived of in an introverted, emotional, and individualistic way. This trend developed in the Scottish and Dutch so-called "further Reformation" of the second half of the seventeenth century and in the Methodist and Pietistic movements of the eighteenth century. Subjectivism became dominating. More and more the individual and his religious emotions became an autonomous theme, in the nineteenth century almost detached from the objective deeds of the triune God by which the individual lives.

In the twentieth century, particularly in the period after the Second World War, there was a sharp reaction, especially in European church life and theology. A new christocentric and eschatological approach almost led to the neglection of the individual's needs and salvation. From the brink of subjectivism we shifted to the brink of objectivism. This is not a legitimate position either. Without the individual person as the ultimate receiver and goal of God's deeds, our beloved modern expressions like "mighty acts," "nature and mission of the church," "witness and service," and "eschatological outlook" become empty and meaningless. For several reasons we cannot adopt the presentation of our theme in the post-Reformation period, but even less can we neglect this theme. What we badly need is a reconsideration of the theme of the individual, both in the light of the broad context provided by biblical theology and in the light of modern psychological insights, so far as they help us to a better understanding on this point of the divine revelation.

THE DOMINATING CONCEPT—REGENERATION

To describe the work of the exalted Christ in the life of the individual, we need many different words, according to the variety of expressions and aspects found in the New Testament. We think of words like "election," "vocation," "regeneration," "cleansing," "illumination," "conversion," "justification," "sanctification." The close association of these words expresses the rich variety of the Spirit's work. Systematic theology for its needs must limit this variety to two or three categories. Generally the work of the Spirit is summarized in the twofold concept of justification and sanctification. The danger of the variety as well as of the summary is that the fact that these works are all works of the one Spirit and so basically one work is obscured. Our context demands an emphasis on the unity of these works as the works of one author. Therefore we have to seek a word in which the variety as a variety within a unity can be made clear. In different times different key words have played their role and have often stamped a whole tradition or a whole period. So in the patristic period, on the one hand, words like "illumination" and "knowledge" and, on the other hand, words like "deification" and "immortality" had a central meaning. For Luther "justification" was the key word, as it is still for many. In the Reformed tradition "regeneration" played a major role as a key word. In Methodism and Pietism words like "conversion" and "sanctification" had a similar function. Friedrich Schleiermacher, as well as Abraham Kuyper, continued the Reformed preference for "regeneration"; Karl Barth seems to make "calling" the dominating concept. Evangelical and Pentecostal groups often prefer words like "sanctification" and "filled with the Spirit."

It is quite important what key words we choose, even when we know that such words have only a very limited significance. They tend to control our whole description of the Spirit's work in the individual. Therefore we cannot be careless in our choice. I personally believe that the word which best expresses the unity and the totality of the Spirit's work is the word "regeneration." This choice depends on what we said in the first chapter about the nature of the Spirit. The Spirit is the life-giver; he is God breathing the breath of life into man. That is the essence of his work in redemption as well as in creation. Redemption as the work of the Spirit means "rebirth." The heart of stone is replaced by a heart of flesh (Ezek. 36:26), breath comes into the dry bones (37:10). So we become children of God, not born of the will of man but of God (John 1:13). For "unless one is born anew, he cannot see the kingdom of God" (3:3). "Therefore, if any one is in Christ, he is a new creation" (2 Cor. 5:17), similar to the first creation: "For it is the God who said, 'Let light shine out of darkness,' who has shone in our hearts to give the light of the knowledge of the glory of God in the face of Christ" (2 Cor. 4:6). This light is life, for the Spirit gives life (2 Cor. 3:6). When you were dead, he made you alive (Eph. 2:1). God brought us forth of his own will by the word of truth (James 1:18), by which he has caused us to be born anew to a living hope through the resurrection of Christ (1 Peter 1:3).

These biblical references can easily be multiplied. They are in full agreement with the primitive and essential meaning of the Spirit as the living God who acts in order to transmit his life to his creatures.

Using regeneration as the key word in our context not only makes clear what the nature of the spiritual work in our lives is, but also implies a decision about its origin and its goal. To say first a word about the goal: The word "regeneration" points to conformity with Christ as the goal of the Spirit. Christ himself is our life. We are dead in our sins, but implanted by the Spirit into the life of him who is the firstborn from the dead. Our goal is that we may be glorified with him (Rom. 8:17), be changed into his likeness from one degree of glory to another by the Lord who is the Spirit (2 Cor. 3:18).

The word "regeneration" implies also a clear answer to the

question of origin. It says that our transition from death to life,
our being made alive with Christ, is entirely and exclusively the
work of the Spirit. "For we are his workmanship, created in Christ
Jesus for good works, which God prepared beforehand . . ." (Eph.
2:10; for the origin, nature, and goal of the Spirit's work, see the
whole passage, Eph. 2:1-10). Here we find the main reason why
the Reformed confession has such a preference for regeneration
as a key word and why other confessions sometimes are so hesitant
about emphasizing this word. If a man has to be born anew, he is
merely passive; he cannot contribute in the least to his rebirth; he
must wait for a miracle from above. All kinds of synergism are
excluded. "So it depends not upon man's will or exertion, but upon
God's mercy" (Rom. 9:16).

This strong anti-synergistic position evokes many objections. It
seems to exclude any activity and responsibility on the part of man.
It looks like an invitation to mere passivity. We cannot deny that
this emphasis on the sovereignty of the Spirit in the Reformed
church has often led to such an attitude. In that case a reaction
was bound to come. Since Augustine's time, the emphasis on regenerating grace has summoned as a reaction an emphasis on free
will (liberum arbitrium), or vice versa. During the time of the
Reformation in particular, the relation between the work of the
Spirit and the work of man aroused deep controversies, from
the discussion between Erasmus and Luther over the decisions of
the Tridentine Council to the conflict between Remonstrants and
Contra-Remonstrants and the Canons of Dort. The position of
the Reformers is clear and convincing; but the position of their adversaries is not without convincing power either. Take, for example,
the fourth Tridentine canon on justification: "If some one says that
man's free will, moved and evoked by God, in no way does cooper-
ate by its assent with the evoking and calling God, so that it enables
and prepares itself to obtain the grace of justification, and that this
free will cannot, if it wills, disagree, but as something unanimated
cannot do anything but behave merely passively, he be anathema."
And the Remonstrants in their five articles greatly stressed the fact
that we depend entirely on regenerating grace (as was also confessed by the Tridentine Council); however, they added (in the

fourth article): "but so far as the mode of action of this grace is concerned—it is not irresistible, for about many is written that they have resisted the Holy Spirit, Acts 7:51, and elsewhere in many places."

One party pleaded the cause of the irresistible power of the Spirit, the other the cause of man's responsibility. Both causes are real concerns for the proclamation of the Word of God. Which party was right, which was wrong?

On the level of psychological observation, all those are right who stress man's free will and responsibility. They see as the only alternative a philosophical determinism which they rightly reject.

The Reformers did not speak on the level of psychological observation but of personal confession. For them the philosophical conception of free will was self-evident, but they considered it a minor truth. Confronted with God, man does not confess his free will, but his complete abuse of it. As Calvin expresses it characteristically: "Man will then be spoken of as having this sort of free choice equally of good and evil, but because he acts wicked by will, not by compulsion. Well put, indeed, but what purpose is served by labeling with a proud name such a slight thing?"[1] The reversal of this confession is the praise of God, who by his sovereign grace has saved us against our free will from our evil free will. Therefore: "Let him who boasts, boast of the Lord."

The opponents did not understand this position. They considered it pessimistic and one-sided. They could not hear it as a confession of sin and of grace. Sad to say, the fault was not only made by them but also made by the Reformers. They did not clearly enough avoid the misunderstanding, as if they also were speaking from the viewpoint of psychological observation. So they often used expressions which seemed to characterize them as supporters of determinism. Standing on the same level with their adversaries, they could not evade the suspicion of pessimistic one-sidedness, which prevented them from acknowledging the truth which in a distorted form was hidden in the opposite position: the truth that man acts voluntarily and responsibly and never as a merely passive object of God's deeds.

As soon as we see that the rejection of free will is not a psychological statement, but a personal confession, we discover that this major truth, as Calvin understood it, does not exclude but embraces and supposes the secondary truth of man's free will and responsibility. When we seek our starting point in *liberum arbitrium*, we do so to the detriment of the confession of regenerating grace. When we seek our starting point in this sovereign grace, we discover that this grace does not push away man's freedom, but confirms, evokes, and sanctifies it. We do not co-operate with God on the same level, but we operate through him and under him. He is not the enemy of our freedom. By the very fact of his sovereignty, he is its Creator and Redeemer. As the Canons of Dort express it: "He moves and strengthens the will in such a way, that as a good tree it can bear fruits of good works . . . And so the will, now being renewed, is not only carried and moved by God, but, moved by God, it also works itself. That is why we rightly say that man, by the grace which he has received, believes and converts."[2]

Not until this century has the wide scope of these words been understood. It is up to the Reformed confession to show that the concern for free will and responsibility is nowhere safer than in the confession of God's regenerating sovereignty. As soon as this is fully understood, we may hope that a fruitless, age-old discussion will come to an end.

THE WAY: JUSTIFICATION AND SANCTIFICATION

What we have to investigate now can also be described as "the content of regeneration." I prefer the word "way," however. "Content" is too static a word. Such a static conception of regeneration is exactly what we want to avoid. Rebirth is not an event once and for all, complete in itself; it means that God puts us on a way, as he does in our first birth, which is not complete in itself either, but is the beginning of a way of life.

Usually this way is described in two words: justification and sanctification. Later we shall have to consider whether these two words will suffice. For the time being we stick to this classical concept. There is no doubt, at least, that we need these two words. At the same time, however, we see that this terminology might obscure the unity of the Spirit's work, expressed in the one word "regeneration." The work of the Spirit is one and indivisible. In dogmatics this unity was often neglected or replaced by the treatment of two different realities: justification and sanctification, which were even used sometimes as slogans in opposition to each other. We refuse to do this, reminding ourselves of Calvin's felicitous remark that we have to do with "a twofold grace" (*duplex gratia*)—twofold, but nevertheless a singular. One can ask why then we need two words to describe one undivided reality. We may ask this question again and again in systematic theology: Why predestination and responsibility; Christ as truly God and truly man, as Priest, Prophet, and King; the church as institution and as community, etc.? This multiplicity of words does not deny the unity of God's work but, on the contrary, reflects it. The unity of God's deed is greater than the singularity of our word. To describe it in a not too inadequate way, we need more than one word. But we have to keep the words as close together as possible. More than ever we have to do that here, where it is not our task to deal with justification and sanctification as such, but with their unity in the one work of regeneration.

The goal of the Spirit is the conformity of the brethren to the Firstborn, of the many to the One. To attain this goal we have to be engrafted into our Head. In him our old humanity was put to death and our new humanity was created. In this corporate personality, decisions were made without us, but for us. We have to be brought into a living connection with these decisions. We have to be led to the source of our new life. That happens, according to the New Testament, through baptism and faith. They make us "simultaneous" with the deeds of Christ. In faith we may say that we are crucified with Christ, have died with Christ, are buried with Christ, have been raised with Christ, and are made to sit with Christ in the heavenly places. These words[3] do not describe successive stages of a mystical experience, but they express what we can better call a juridical transaction, an adjudication, a transfer, an appointment. In dogmatical terminology we speak of "imputation," which is the reverse of the imputation of our sinful existence which Christ has taken upon himself. Through faith in the work of the

One-for-all, God declares us to be brethren of Christ, adopted
children, righteous, without spot or wrinkle, heirs of the Kingdom.
Since the days of Paul, we describe this miracle in juridical terms,
as an act of "justification," to express the fact that we are not dealing with our own meritorious acts or with mystical experiences, but
with a divine initiative, coming from outside; a declaration; a one-
sided act of reconciliation, which restores the broken relation between God and us.

This way of describing the rebirth of man is fundamental. It is
not complete, however. A declaration, an appointment, etc., are not
mere words; they change relations, and therefore they also change
the men involved in these relations. In God's case, that is not only
a subsequent fact—it is his aim that men should be changed according to the image of his Son. We are engrafted in order that we may
grow. We are appointed in order that we may follow a new calling.
We are adopted as sons in order that we may behave as sons. The
work *pro nobis* seeks a follow-up in the work *in nobis*. Even this
way of expressing the togetherness of justification and sanctification is dangerous, however. It suggests two more or less connected
successive acts; but we are dealing with one and the same movement. God's Word is always a creative act. In calling us his sons, he
makes us behave as sons. In creating a new relation, he creates a
new being. It is really one twofold grace. In that one grace, justification and sanctification are not two parts; in the one event they
are related as fundament and goal, as root and fruit. Our regeneration is that we are engrafted into Christ in such a way that we become changed according to his image.

I assume that we all more or less agree about this unity of justification and sanctification. However, as soon as we try to formulate
this connection more precisely, new differences arise. On the one
hand, I think of a man like the great Reformed preacher Kohlbrugge (1803-1875), for whom the justification of the ungodly was
the one and the all of the Word of God. He disliked exhortations
to sanctification, because he was afraid that this would lead to self-
salvation and Phariseeism. For him the main sin was man's pride,
his rebellious inclination to take his salvation in his own hands.
Man has nothing to do except to stick to his justification, to believe

that Christ has done all for him and that the only thing we can do is to be grateful. It was Kohlbrugge's confidence that such an attitude of faith would be the most fertile soil for real good works.

On the other hand, I think of a man like John Wesley (1703-1791), to whom justification by faith alone was a living reality, but who made a sharp distinction between justification and sanctification and who saw as the goal to be pursued seriously by every Christian: to put on love as the bond of perfection. Continuous exhortation to holiness was at the center of his preaching. He believed in "inherent perfection," i.e., in the perfectability of the faithful in this life.

Kohlbrugge and Wesley would have abhorred one another's preaching. In my opinion dogmatical theology should not decide in favor of one or the other. It ought to remind us, instead, of three facts. First: Sin manifests itself in different forms. Sin can have the form of pride, Phariseeism, self-salvation. Sin can also have the form of slowness and quietism. These different forms demand different emphases. Second: We have to remind one another that the first emphasis brings us very near to antinomianism and quietism, and the second to legalism and self-salvation. Third: Both approaches have to be understood as complementary. Faith in Christ without love is dead, is a pseudo-faith. And a sanctification which is not rooted in gratitude for justification is but a kind of Christian personality-culture. We easily forget that the two words "justification" and "sanctification" do not describe different spiritual stages or situations, but are in their togetherness an attempt to point from two sides, from the basis and from the goal, to the movement in which the Holy Spirit involves us: the movement toward our Redeemer, in order to be changed according to his image. That is the movement of our rebirth.

THE WAY: DYING AND RISING WITH CHRIST

We need yet another pair of words to describe the movement of regeneration, i.e., the words "dying" and "rising" with Christ, *mortificatio* and *vivificatio*. They can in no way be identified with *iustificatio* and *sanctificatio*. For some time now they have not played an important role in systematic theology, a fact which has had a harmful influence on the life of the church.

In the time of the Reformation these words were used frequently. Luther and the Lutheran reformation were not so familiar with this terminology. Luther himself preferred words like *opus alienum* and *opus proprium*. Calvin and the Reformed tradition, on the contrary, used the words "mortification" and "vivification" as fixed terms in their pneumatology. The difference on this point between Lutherans and Reformed is not only a matter of phraseology, but also of content. In the Lutheran tradition the words are used in terms of justification: Our dying is our contrition and repentance; our rising is our joyful faith in the justifying Christ. In the Reformed tradition the words are used in terms of sanctification: Our dying is our continuous self-renunciation and our daily struggle against our sinful ego; our rising is our walking in newness of life, our putting on the new man, re-created after the image of God.[4] Calvin sometimes gives the impression that dying and rising are successive acts, but the common opinion is that they are simultaneous and that they are one another's reverse.[5]

The Heidelberg Catechism combines the Lutheran and the Reformed emphases in questions and answers 88-90. To the question: "*What is the dying of the old self?*" it answers: "Sincere sorrow over our sins and more and more to hate them and to flee from them"; and to the question: "*What is the birth of the new man?*" it answers: "Complete joy in God through Christ and a strong desire to live according to the will of God in all good works." As so often, the Heidelberg Catechism by intuition has given the right solution. Mortification and justification are another way to describe the whole way of regeneration. They are as embracing as the words "justification" and "sanctification" are, now from another angle; their scope can only be made clear if we connect both with justification as well as with sanctification.

Our *justification* is a reality of dying and rising with Christ. In the event of justification we are crucified, we die, and we are buried with Christ. In the act of faith we identify ourselves with the suffering Christ who was made to be sin for our sake; we confess that our sinful life was nullified in his death. At the same time we know that he who died in our place was raised on behalf of us, that in a narrow escape our rejected humanity was adopted and renewed, that we have a new life in Christ. Paul's words—about the old man whom we have to put off and the new man, created after the likeness of God, whom we have to put on—are primarily spoken in view of the old and the new man in Christ, and in view of us only insofar as we, by act of repentance and faith, are identified with him as our Representative.[6]

Paul does not speak only of repentance and faith in this context, but also of baptism, especially in Romans 6 and Colossians 2. The most adequate rite is baptism by immersion, in which according to Paul we are drowned with Christ and also raised with him. This does not happen automatically. In Colossians 2:12, Paul adds the words "through faith in the working of God, who raised him from the dead." Baptism is not an automatic thing, but neither is it merely symbolic, at any rate not in the sense in which we use the word "symbolic." Baptism is a seal, a confirmation, a realization of our dying and rising with Christ in terms of justification, for in baptism his crucifixion and resurrection are made present in our lives; "we have been united with him in a death like his" (Rom. 6:5). "So you also must consider yourselves dead to sin and alive to God in Christ Jesus" (vs. 11). This means: Our faith is founded on what happened in our baptism. It is a constant repentant "no" to what we are in ourselves and a constant joyful "yes" to the adjudication of the new humanity in Christ.

Our *sanctification* also is a reality of dying and rising with Christ, because sanctification is nothing else than the reality of justification applied to (by God) and taken seriously (by ourselves) in the reality of our life. First, sanctification means that we take seriously that our egotistic and worldly-minded existences are declared void in Christ's sacrifice; as a consequence, we must struggle with ourselves in order to kill what we know to be invalid and rejected. Dying with Christ means constant self-denial, or as Jesus calls it: to take up our cross. This expression does not deal with our willingness to undergo sufferings and sorrow which come to us against our will, but to undertake in the power of the Spirit a war

against ourselves. It is very meaningful that Jesus is said to have
used this expression right after the announcement of his own cross
(Mark 8:31-34). Paul speaks about the same reality as a fight between the Holy Spirit in us and our flesh, that is, our sinful nature
with its pride and desires (Gal. 5:17-26). Although in this fight
the Spirit often seems to get the worst of it, this very fight is the
sign of the Spirit's presence in our lives. The Spirit is absent when
we stop fighting, not when we lose. Often we must say: "Wretched
man that I am! Who will deliver me from this body of death?";
but looking to our risen Representative, who is the guarantee of
our victory, we may also say: "Thanks be to God through Jesus
Christ our Lord!" (Rom. 7:24-25). With God's power we again
and again (and even as Calvin prefers to say: "more and more"),
in our decisions and behavior, express our desire to live in the joyful
style of Christ's new humanity, to acknowledge his seemingly fool-
ish way as the way of true wisdom and life. That is our rising with
Christ. In this life it is but very partial. Paul speaks of it more in
terms of exhortations than of descriptions. As the Heidelberg Catechism says, "even the holiest make only a small beginning in obedience in this life" (Answer 114). Nevertheless it is a real beginning
in which we begin to "know him and the power of his resurrection" (Phil. 3:10).

Mortification and vivification have yet a third aspect which
cannot be described in terms of justification or sanctification, but
only in terms of *vocation*, of the relation of the Christian and the
church toward the world. Dying with Christ does not only mean
that we see through ourselves, but also through the world around
us with its pride, vanity, and idolatry, so that "the world has been
crucified to me and I to the world." As a consequence of it we are
urged to deviate from the ways of the world around us on decisive
points. Such non-conformity (not as an end in itself, but as the reverse of the conformity with Christ) necessarily evokes alienation
from our surroundings and under special circumstances leads to
oppression and even martyrdom. The disciple of Christ may know
that in this way he shares the cross of Christ. It is especially Paul
who, writing about his afflictions in the Second Letter to the Corinthians, has found deep and strong words to express the meaning

of dying and rising with Christ in this respect. He describes it in
these words: "We are afflicted in every way, but not crushed; per-
plexed, but not driven to despair; persecuted, but not forsaken;
struck down, but not destroyed; always carrying in the body the
death of Jesus, so that the life of Jesus may also be manifested in
our bodies." And elsewhere he describes himself "as dying, and
behold we live . . . as sorrowful, yet always rejoicing."[7] The reality
and the meaning of how Christ, through his Spirit, leads his followers in conformity with his way is hardly explored in the teaching
of the church and hardly formulated in systematic terms. In the
New Testament and especially in Paul and John, this aspect is
quite essential. A deeper consideration of it would help many individual Christians as well as the church as a whole to a deeper
understanding and a more joyful acceptance of their way in the
world.

The Spirit grants us rebirth, creates in us a new way of life. It
is a real way: from justification to sanctification, from mortification
to vivification. We never leave this beginning behind us, for again
and again renewed faith in our justification is the only sufficient
power of our sanctification. And mortification is always the reverse
and the outside of vivification; we rise to the extent of our dying.
While in this life we have never left the beginning behind us, we
always have the end still ahead of us. The goal of this way is never
attained in life. However, we may believe that in this mysterious
process "we are being changed into the likeness of Christ, for this
comes from the Lord who is the Spirit."

REGENERATION AND EXPERIENCE

As a kind of appendix to the main lines drawn in the previous
pages, we will mention an aspect of individual pneumatology which
has been of great importance in church history and to which a
special systematic attention was given in Reformed theology. I
mean: the place of experience (German: *Erfahrung*; Dutch: *be-
vinding*) in the regenerating work of the Spirit. The questions are:
Is the work of the Spirit a reality which we can only believe ac-

cording to God's promises? Or do we consciously experience it? And
if so, how do we experience it? And last but not least, can this experience serve as an evidence of the Spirit's presence? All these
theological questions find their common root in the often anxious
questions which every true believer in due time puts to himself:
How do I know that I am a child of God? What are the signs
from which I can conclude that the Spirit dwells in me?

First we must remark that the presence of the Spirit, as well
as the creation of the world, the incarnation, and the atonement,
is an object of faith in the Word of God which demands our acceptance and confidence. Faith is the conviction of things not seen.
That does not imply, however, that faith and experience exclude
one another. Faith affects the whole of our existence and so brings
with it its own kind of experience. So far there is a high measure of
agreement. Differences arise only when the question is asked, What
is this kind of experience?

Some theologians and pastors emphasize what we may call the
"intentional" character of faith. The nature of faith is that it is
entirely occupied by its object. Faith (*pistis, fides*) is an act of confidence in God's fidelity; it is saying "Amen" to the promises of
God (Hebrew: *amunah*). The faithful person is freed from himself, from his introversion, from his pressure to do something and
to be something. He lives by the grace of the Other. He "ex-ists,"
which means, literally, "he treads out of himself." We find this
emphasis especially in Luther, in Kohlbrugge, and in Barth. To
show the biblical and pastoral strength of this position, I must
recommend the reading of Kohlbrugge's sermons and other writings. Being asked when and where his conversion took place, he
answered: "On Golgotha!" In one of his books he speaks of the
signs of election in our lives and asks: "From what facts can I conclude that I am elected?" His answer is simply: "the publican was
standing far off." He also asks: "To what little word do you have to
stick when you feel you cannot find a single sign of true grace in
yourself and when you are deeply dejected about that?" The short
answer is: "Stick to the little word: 'Nevertheless.' "[8]

This position is wholesome as long as it applies to people who
are anxious about their salvation and who try to build their cer-

tainty upon the sand of their sentiments and inner experiences. As soon as it is addressed to people who do not share this anxiety, it leads to a mere external and objectivistic and often even intellectualistic acceptance of the truth of grace. In that case reaction is bound to come, because faith, on the one hand, is the liberation from our own natural religious experiences but, on the other hand, faith creates new spiritual experiences as the fruits of the Spirit's regenerating power. In my opinion, it is to a large extent possible to describe the history of the Western church in terms of this problem. The old Germanic faith was objectivistic with a prevalence of military terminology (see the Saxon poem *Heliand*). Bernard of Clairvaux and the piety of the Crusaders made the relation to Christ far more personal and intimate. At the end of the Middle Ages this led to an introverted moralism and mysticism to which Luther's preaching of justification by faith alone brought the true remedy. After less than a century this developed into such an intellectualistic objectivism and new kind of scholasticism that first the "further Reformation" in Scotland and the Netherlands, and afterward German Pietism and English Methodism, formed a highly necessary corrective. In the eighteenth and nineteenth centuries, this development led to different kinds of pietistic and liberal subjectivism. Theology after the First World War formed a strong reaction against this subjectivism. The objectivism to which this new trend can lead has been heavily attacked in the last decades by the school of Bultmann and other groups.

If we try to describe the legitimate content and place of experience in the work of the Spirit, we look to the first century of our Reformed confession, in which this problem was deeply considered. More than the Lutherans, the Reformed were inclined to give room to experience as a result of regeneration. They sought that room in two directions. They saw regeneration working either primarily in good works, in deeds of love, or primarily in the personal, inner experiences. The first we call the ethical experience, the second the mystical experience. The interest in this problem has a special background and tendency in the Reformed tradition. The preponderance of predestination in Reformed teaching since the second half of the sixteenth century inevitably led to the quest of reliable signs of our personal election, which were expected to be found in the realm of experience. Our ancestors expressed this problem in the very inadequate words *syllogismus practicus*, which mean: a syllogism, a sound argument, based on practice, on the acts or experiences of our real life. The word "syllogism" is wrong, because we do not deal here with logical conclusions, but with an act of the Spirit who in special deeds or experiences bears witness that we are children of God.

The classical expression of the *syllogismus practicus* in the field of *ethical experience* is found in the Heidelberg Catechism, Answer 86, which, as one of the reasons for doing good works, mentions: "that we ourselves may be assured of our faith by its fruits." This thought is often attacked as a kind of circular argument, suggesting that only faith can distinguish the works of faith, so that faith could confirm itself by itself. But the question is not as simple as that. We think of words in the First Letter of John like "And by this we may be sure that we know him, if we keep his commandments" (2:3) and "We know that we have passed out of death into life, because we love the brethren" (3:14; cf. 3:24). The Reformers frequently quoted in this connection 2 Peter 1:10: "Therefore, brethren, be the more zealous to confirm your call and election . . ." Calvin has devoted some careful paragraphs in his *Institutes* to the question: Can our works supply evidence for our childhood of God? According to Niesel, Calvin rejects the *syllogismus practicus*; according to Vander Linde and Krusche, who both wrote books on Calvin's pneumatology, Calvin accepts the *syllogismus practicus*.[9] I agree with this last conclusion. The reason for doubt lies in the fact that Calvin's exposition is very careful and very well balanced. He strongly denies that we can rest on our works for the certainty of our salvation; but, as he says, the works are "complements," "testimonies of God's dwelling and governing in us." They form an a posteriori comfort for the faithful and as such, as he expresses it in his comment on 1 John 4:17, they function as a kind of *secundarium adminiculum*, though he quickly adds: "but in the meantime we must be founded in grace alone."

We should acknowledge that the *syllogismus ethicus* points to a reality. The power of regeneration is revealed in the fact that it urges us, to our own surprise and against our fleshly nature, to do and to say things which are according to God's will. Such fruits never give reason for pride, only for humble gratitude. They are additional signs that God has not passed over us with his grace. They confirm a knowledge which primarily and essentially comes to us not in our ethical experience (which at the best is a very ambiguous experience) but in God's Word and promises.[10]

After some decades the *syllogismus ethicus* had to yield the pastoral and theological interest to the *mystical experience*. That shift in attention was connected with the wave of inner mystical religiosity in all the European churches, the Roman Catholic Church in the front, in the seventeenth century. In the Reformed church the question now is: Are there inner experiences which can encourage the seeker, for certain, that he is included in the eternal decree? The classical document of the *syllogismus mysticus* is the Canons of Dort. Here we find the words: "the elect . . . attain the assurance of this eternal and unchangeable election . . . by observing in themselves, with a spiritual joy and holy pleasure, the infallible fruits of election pointed out in the Word of God, i.e. true faith in Christ, childlike fear of God, godly grief about sin, hunger and thirst for righteousness, and so on" (I, 12). Characteristic also are the words that the faithful reassure themselves in the fact "that they know and feel that they by this grace of God wholeheartedly believe and love their Savior" (III, 13). The first passage mentions, as scriptural evidence, 2 Corinthians 13:5: "Examine yourselves, to see whether you are holding to your faith. Test yourselves." This is the answer to a different question, however, as the context and the commentaries can teach us. Other evidences are not mentioned, and it is hard to find them. Calvin, who speaks about the *syllogismus ethicus,* is silent about the *syllogismus mysticus.* Nevertheless the last has had far more influence on Reformed piety than the first.[11] That fact has its confessional and cultural reasons; we must deplore it, however. We heard the Canons of Dort say that we have to observe in ourselves our faith in Christ. But faith is not something to be observed but to be done. They invite us even to observe with joy and pleasure our grief about sin. Can we suffer from our sin and at the same time observe that suffering with pleasure? That looks like schizophrenia. They state also that we "know and feel" that we believe and love. But as soon as we try to feel our love, we no longer actually love. The Canons of Dort inaugurated a long period of unprofitable introversion, the aftermath of which is still felt in many corners of the Reformed church.

When we are opposed to the *syllogismus mysticus*, we are so primarily for theological reasons but, in addition, for psychological reasons. For many centuries European Christendom held a substantialistic conception of man, inherited from Greco-Roman philosophy. Man was conceived of as an autonomous, self-centered, individual entity, an inner life consisting of intellect and will, or later: intellect, will, and feeling. Only after a very long time did we discover that the Bible does not share this view, but replaces our substantialistic view by a relationalistic one: Man is what he is not by his inner life, but by his relations to God, his neighbor, and the world around him. This view is now common in twentieth-century anthropology. It puts an end to many traditional elements in individual pneumatology. Words like *gratia infusa*, "new qualities" (Canons of Dort III, 11), and many others can no longer be used. We think of regeneration not so much in terms of a renewal of an inner substance (let alone in terms of our sentiments) as in terms of a renewed relation to God and our neighbor. That demands a complete rethinking of individual pneumatology, a common task of theologians and pastors which is still ahead of us.

To return now to the relation of regeneration and experience, we must say that the relational categories of the Reformers, Kohlbrugge, and twentieth-century theology appeal far more to us than the categories of introversion and substance of the seventeenth to nineteenth centuries. At the same time we know that nothing is real which does not function. Therefore we cannot get rid of the problems of our ancestors, who asked how our relation to Christ works in our lives. But we have to keep in mind that only the relation to our crucified and risen Representative can create renewing experiences, mostly of an ethical and sometimes also of a mystical kind. Only if we forget ourselves with all our experiences, in favor of our Redeemer, can such experiences of renewal arise. The more we

forget ourselves and look to Christ, the more we are filled with his
love and the more we are regenerated to a new life.[12]

A THIRD ELEMENT IN REGENERATION?

As we mentioned before, dogmatics traditionally speaks about
regeneration in a twofold way: justification and sanctification. This
division has been challenged, however, since the Revivalist and
Pentecostal movements began. These movements experienced still
another blessing of the Holy Spirit in the life of the individual,
which is now widely known as the "filling by the Holy Spirit" or
"the baptism by the Holy Spirit." So these groups believe in a
threefold work of the Spirit: justification, sanctification, and being
filled by the Spirit.

Official theology, so far as I know, has until now paid hardly
any attention to this Revivalist conviction. Small wonder, because
there is a watertight partition-wall between these groups and theology in seminaries and universities. I believe that this partition
is to the detriment of both parties, and I will make an attempt to
break through the wall. I do so although I am aware of the fact
that I set foot on an unexplored field and that my thoughts here,
even more than those on other aspects of my theme, must be considered as preliminary and needing correction by others.

The first question is: Are there sound reasons for assuming such
a third element in the Spirit's work? The groups mentioned have
many biblical words available to give a positive answer to that question. They point to the promise of John the Baptist—that Christ
will baptize with the Holy Spirit and with fire—a promise which
is repeated in the prologue of Acts and which, by its author, is considered as having been fulfilled in the great events of Pentecost and
also in many other events mentioned later on. The book of Acts is
indeed the main source for a doctrine of a third aspect of the Spirit's
work. The disciples on whom the Spirit fell were faithful believers
even before this event. They had already had an experience of
discipleship, i.e., of justification and sanctification. Nevertheless,
they were in need of more; they needed, as Luke says, to be filled

with the Holy Spirit.[13] This and similar expressions are frequent
in the Lukan writings. Besides their use in Acts 2, three other passages in which they appear are often quoted by the Pentecostal
groups, that is, Acts 8:14-17; 10:44-46; and 19:6. The first speaks
about Samaritans who had received the Word of God and were
baptized, but the Spirit "had not yet fallen on any of them." So
Peter and John came, and after prayer and laying on of hands, the
Samaritans "received the Holy Spirit." The second passage describes how the Spirit fell on Cornelius and other proselytes: "For
they heard them speaking in tongues and extolling God." The third
passage speaks about Gentiles, real disciples of Jesus, who are asked
by Paul: "Did you receive the Holy Spirit when you believed?" and
who said they had not. After baptism and the laying on of hands
by Paul, "the Holy Spirit came on them; and they spoke with
tongues and prophesied." As we see, there are differences among
the three reports. Twice we hear of an interval between conversion
and the receiving of the Spirit. Once (in Acts 10) they seem to be
simultaneous. In that case baptism follows; in the other cases it
comes before. The laying on of hands is mentioned as necessary in
two cases and did not happen in one case. Consequently, important details are unclear. Nevertheless, the main line is clear: By a
special working of the Spirit, the faithful are empowered to speak
in tongues, to prophesy, to praise God, that is, to give a powerful
expression of God's mighty acts to those around them.

The other book to which the Revivalist and Pentecostal groups
appeal is 1 Corinthians, Paul's treatment of the *charismata*, the
spiritual gifts (1 Cor. 12-14). Like the passages in Acts, it also mentions prophecy and speaking in tongues as special gifts of the
Spirit. According to Paul, every faithful Christian, in addition to
faith, hope, and love (or: to justification and sanctification), re-
ceives from the Spirit a special gift for the upbuilding of the body
of Christ. In the enumeration of gifts in 1 Corinthians 12:8-11 (a
basic passage for the Pentecostal movement), Paul mentions: utter-
ance of wisdom and of knowledge, faith, gifts of healing, working
of miracles (especially casting out of demons), prophecy, the test-
ing of prophets, the speaking in various kinds of languages, and
the interpretation of these languages. In this connection Paul

fights on two fronts: On the one hand, he encourages the Corinthians earnestly to desire these spiritual gifts; on the other hand, he warns them that the gifts are useless, and even harmful, if not controlled by love, that is, if not used for humble service to the less-gifted members of the body. Paul does not use the filling terminology as Luke does, but we have the impression that he points to the same or similar facts. For him also the work of the Spirit is not exhausted in justification and sanctification; an additional working is promised and must therefore be sought. All this leads us to the conclusion that the Pentecostals are basically right when they speak of a working of the Holy Spirit beyond that which is acknowledged in the major denominations.

Things become complicated, however, when we try to systematize these biblical data in one way or another. The Pentecostals are fundamentalists who harmonize the underlying texts at all costs. A systematic theologian has to seek for a deeper cohesion and tendency, which explain the differences instead of explaining them away. For, no doubt, deep differences exist between Acts and Paul's letters, and the way in which we deal with them is decisive for the whole subject. We have already seen that the typical Lukan terminology is absent in Paul. A more careful analysis of all the passages in Paul dealing with the *charismata* proves that for Paul this special working of the Spirit includes also teaching and administration (1 Cor. 12:28), service, aid, mercy, and exhortation (Rom. 12:6-8). For Luke, the speaking in tongues, i.e., in unknown languages, is the central gift. For Paul, on the contrary, it is a phenomenon on the fringe, almost useless; for him prophecy is in the center. Another difference is that Paul never speaks of this work of the Spirit as a second act, which can come after an interval; for him this third gift belongs to the others and forms a unity with them.

These differences are so great that we are almost inclined to believe that Luke and Paul speak about different things. That conclusion would, however, neglect the not less striking correspondence. My explanation of the difference is this: Luke speaks as a historian; he wants to describe how the gospel made its way from Jerusalem and Judea to Samaria and to the ends of the earth. In connection with this purpose, he describes, at four different times, a breakthrough of the Spirit, and he does so in terms of being filled by the Spirit, of speaking in tongues, and prophesying. The first breakthrough was on the day of Pentecost in Jerusalem (ch. 2), the second in Samaria (ch. 8), the third under those "who feared God," the proselytes (ch. 10), and the fourth in the pagan world of Ephesus (ch. 19). The last three can be considered as reiterations of Pentecost, as is explicitly said by Peter in the case of Cornelius (10:47; 11:15). Luke's high capacities as a composer and a historian of the Greek style are evident in these stories. We cannot use them for a direct application in systematic theology. We can assume, however, that Luke would not have given the descriptions in this way unless he knew that parallel phenomena belonged to the life of the Christian congregations for which he wrote.

Luke's teacher Paul tells us what these parallel phenomena were in 1 Corinthians 12 and 14. Unlike Luke, his aim is not to give historical information, but pastoral guidance. In Corinth Paul found the development and the corruption of a tradition of which Luke had outlined the origins. Enthusiasm had led to loveless pride and to chaos. In that situation Paul develops what we may call a theology of the filling by the Spirit. Not all the historical facts of the beginning can find a place in this normative conception which was meant for church life in established congregations. A new well always begins with a vehement spouting-up of water; after that it creates a more steady and quiet stream. Some want the spouting-up to be continued. Others believe that the well stopped because the spouting-up stopped. Paul thinks along a third line. Systematic theology has to follow his reflections. We reject, on the one hand, the neglect of these thoughts by the official churches and, on the other hand, the Pentecostal theology which takes its starting point not in Paul's reflections but in Luke's descriptions.

THE NATURE OF THE THIRD GIFT

To understand the nature of the third gift, we have to look at an emphasis which is common to Luke and Paul: the emphasis on the effect of the filling, the effect of the *charismata*. Whenever

Luke, in his Gospel or in Acts, speaks of being filled with the Spirit, he lays full emphasis not on the inner emotions caused by this event, but on its external consequences: People begin to prophesy, to exclaim, to praise God, to be Christ's witnesses, to speak in tongues, to testify to the enemies, to speak the Word of God with boldness, to proclaim Jesus. All these expressions are used by Luke in connection with the filling by the Holy Spirit, which without any exception is seen as a power directed toward communication with others. The same holds true for Paul. His standard for judging the value of the *charismata* is whether or not they are directed toward what he calls "the edification (*oikodome*) of the church." He develops this standard mainly in 1 Corinthians 14, but Romans 12:4-9 is also a clear statement of this point of view. The *charismata* are gifts to the individuals, but they are never meant for private use. Instead they are meant to benefit the body as a whole, and (we must add in view of 1 Cor. 14:23-25) in this way they are also a missionary witness to the world. Only "when each part is working properly," "the whole body . . . makes bodily growth and upbuilds itself in love" (Eph. 4:16). Or, as 1 Corinthians 13 puts it: without love (i.e., the love of Christ and of the other members of the body), all the spiritual gifts are useless.

It is clear that being filled by the Spirit means to equip the individual in such a way that he becomes an instrument for the ongoing process of the Spirit in the church and in the world. It is more than what is expressed in sanctification which makes us, in love and in good works, a testimony of Christ to our neighbor. This is a common command, related to our common human nature, which can be carried out in a person to person relation. Therefore, in addition to the *fruits* of the Spirit—faith, hope, love—there are also the *gifts* of the Spirit, which vary from one member to another and which are the instruments by which we partake in the wider ecclesiastical and cosmic dimensions of the Spirit's work. The filling by the Spirit means that the justified and sanctified are now turned, so to speak, inside out. In Acts they are turned primarily to the world; in Paul primarily to the total body of Christ; but this is merely a difference in situation and emphasis. Luke calls it "being filled," and in Ephesians 4 Paul mentions it in connection with growth and mature manhood, and rightly so; for, as we all know, in natural life we cannot adequately express and communicate our experiences unless they have become an integral part of ourselves. The power to partake of that which the Spirit has granted to us, in the wider context of his work in humanity, is the sign of spiritual maturity. Such maturity has to do with the mystery of our individuality. The Spirit in justification occupies the center of ourselves; in sanctification, the whole circle of our human nature; and in filling us, he occupies our individuality, the special mark which I and I alone bear, the special contribution which I have to make to the whole of life. He takes it up for the whole of the Kingdom of God.

In defining the third gift in this way, we have decided some questions on which Luke the historian and Paul the Apostle seem to differ. In Acts the *charismata* seem to be purely supernatural; in Paul, especially in Romans 12, it is clear that they are closely related to natural gifts which now are taken into the service of the Lord. In Acts the *charismata* seem to be mainly ecstatic, out of human control; in Paul we see that the faithful have them under control: "the spirits of prophets are subject to prophets" (1 Cor. 14:32). In Acts it seems that we cannot influence the reception of special *charismata*; in Paul we see that we not only can but must "earnestly desire the spiritual gifts" (1 Cor. 12:31; 14:1).

At the beginning of this section, I said that official theology has neglected this aspect of the Spirit's work. Now I must make one important exception, namely, Karl Barth in the last volume of his *Church Dogmatics* (IV, 3). After having dealt with justification in IV, 1, and with sanctification in IV, 2, he introduces a third aspect, that of "calling." The justified and sanctified Christian is now called to participate in the work of Christ, that is: to be a witness. In another connection, I dealt with the way in which Barth extols calling above personal salvation. Here we stress the fact that Barth is aware of a third dimension in pneumatology. Although he only incidentally relates his discovery to the biblical data with which we deal here and with the concern of the Revivalists and Pentecostals, I see in his line of thought great perspectives for the things which occupy us here.

THE VARIETY OF THE CHARISMATA

According to what just has been said, the variety of the spiritual gifts must correspond to the variety of the individuals. In five passages Paul gives a kind of enumeration of the *charismata*: Romans 12:6-8; 1 Corinthians 12:8-10, 28; 14:6; Ephesians 4:11. These lists overlap one another, but are far from identical. Particularly striking is the difference between the more ordinary gifts in Romans 12:6-8 and the more extraordinary ones in 1 Corinthians 12:8-10. Paul had to oppose a tendency in Corinth which led to greater uniformity in favor of some sensational *charismata*. With all his apostolic authority, he defends the variety in which there is also room for less spectacular gifts. He even changes from the defense to the attack. What was considered as the highest gift—speaking in unknown languages—Paul puts on the lowest level, because it is of no use to the upbuilding of the body. The so-called glossolalia was a widespread religious phenomenon in the ancient world. Paul probably alludes to it when he says: "When you were still pagan, you were swept off to those dumb heathen gods" (1 Cor. 12:2, N.E.B.), and he reminds them of the fact that ecstasy as such is not a sign of the Spirit, because people in such ecstasy even can say: "Jesus is cursed!" Paul himself possesses the gift of glossolalia (14:8), but he shrinks from admitting in the congregation signs of ecstasy in which, as he puts it, spirit and mind no longer go together (14:12 ff.). Glossolalia needs interpretation; otherwise it is not to the upbuilding of the body. As a *charisma* it falls far behind helping, administration, teaching, and serving. The best Paul can say is: "Do not forbid speaking in tongues" (14:39).

In the same verse he says: "earnestly desire to prophesy." Paul sees prophecy as the highest gift of all. We badly need a study of the content and the theological relevance of New Testament prophecy. In this context I cannot say more than that in my opinion prophecy is the gift of understanding and expressing what the will of God is for a given present situation.[14] How greatly we long for that *charisma* in our days with their many challenges and confusions! Are we sure that the church of today lacks this gift? Probably we have prophets in our midst, on the smaller and broader levels of our church life. It is possible that we do not recognize them and treat their insights and warnings as just one more private opinion. The primitive church was in the opposite danger. It held prophecy in such a high esteem that it did not sufficiently distinguish between true and false prophecy. Therefore, Paul also mentions as a *charisma* "the ability to distinguish between spirits" (12:10). The abuse, especially as it was found in the Montanist movement, has caused the withering of this gift. But, as the Romans rightly said: *abusus non tollit usum.* The fault which the primitive and the present church have in common is that both are inclined to treat prophecy as an individualistic gift; but it is meant to be used and to be tested by the church as a whole.

In this connection I cannot deal with all the *charismata* which Paul enumerates. Of some of them the meaning is even obscure. A specific treatment in our context is not necessary, because by their very nature they vary according to the individual capacity, the historic and local situation, and the needs of the body of Christ and of the world.

TRUTH AND UNTRUTH IN THE CHURCHES AND THE SECTS

Finally we must say something about the consequence of all this for the opposition between the churches and the Pentecostal movement. Let us begin with what is easiest to us: to point out where the latter deviates from what we consider to be the normative line in the New Testament. First, as we saw, Pentecostals interpret Paul in the light of Luke, instead of the other way round, which is not a sound hermeneutical procedure. In Paul they focus almost exclusively on 1 Corinthians 12:7-11, which they wrongly consider as a systematic and complete presentation of the *charismata.* Consequently, to the same extent they neglect the less sensational gifts which Paul mentions in other passages. Besides that, they pay the highest attention to the speaking in unknown languages, which in Paul's eyes is only a gift of minor importance. Finally, this special attention depends on the fact that in these groups the gifts are considered more as signs of God's grace toward the individual than as instruments in the service of those who lack these gifts. For all these reasons, the church cannot accept the Pentecostal presentation of the work of the Spirit. It is her calling to plead the cause of those who received less sensational gifts and to emphasize that all practice of the gifts has to be controlled by love and has to aim at the upbuilding of the body of Christ as a whole.

At the same time, the "non-Pentecostal" churches have to hear in the Pentecostal movement God summoning us, not to quench the Spirit and earnestly to desire the spiritual gifts. What did we do with 1 Corinthians 12-14? Where do we show to the Pentecostals, and to the world around us, that our members serve one another in such a way that we grow up in every way into Christ, to the mature manhood? The Pentecostal movement is God's judgment upon a church which lost its inner growth and its outward extension, its character as a vertical as well as a horizontal movement. We have to rediscover the meaning of the variety of the spiritual gifts. We are not to copy the situation in Corinth, let alone that on the day of Pentecost. We have to interpret the gifts in the light of Paul's teaching into the patterns and needs of the life of today. In order to achieve that, we have a long way of common thinking and praying before us. On that way we must be willing to learn as much as we can from the Pentecostals. In our congregational life we must start with the strong conviction that every one who loves Christ has to make a specific contribution to the growth of our common life. Gifts of simple service in seemingly little details are as much needed as gifts of administration, social activity, and teaching. In the awareness that every member has a contribution to make, the European churches have much to learn from those of North America. At the same time we have to rediscover together some badly neglected gifts, primarily the gift of prophecy. Only when we earnestly desire the spiritual gifts, will God grant us the solution of many problems with which we now wrestle: the role of the laity, the common testimony in social and political matters, the missionary power and missionary structure of the congregation, the visible unity of the church.

V

THE SPIRIT, THE WORLD,
AND THE CONSUMMATION

In this chapter we turn to the widest perspectives of the Spirit's work, in the creation and re-creation of the world. These aspects can in no sense be an appendix to what has been said before. Insofar as the Spirit is the name of God in action, nothing short of the whole creation can be the field of his operation. And insofar as the Spirit is the name of the exalted Christ in action, the same holds true, because Christ is meant as the Savior of the world and the Head of all mankind. We had to begin with this idea when, first of all in Chapter II, we dealt with the mission as the Spirit's primary work. In that chapter the world was only considered as the field of the Spirit's operation. Speaking about the church and the individual, we tried to describe the first results, the first fruits of the Spirit in the world. Now we have to see what the cosmic fruits of Christ's Spirit are. We will close with the eschatological fruits. Before we have to see what the present fruits of Christ's Spirit are. That will occupy us in the middle part of this chapter. We cannot do so, however, if we have not first dealt with the mode and the results of the Spirit's action, before Christ and apart from the exalted Christ, in the world and in the history of Israel. In this widest circumference these three themes, all more or less neglected in our traditional theology, belong together.

THE SPIRIT IN CREATION AND PRESERVATION

From the viewpoint of logical order, it seems unwise to deal with creation and the world after Christ and the church. This is the order of biblical thinking, however. God's relation to creation is not the starting point, but the widest perspective of Israel's faith.

It is the conviction of those who witness in the Scriptures that we have no direct access to God's work in creation. The world as we know it is ambiguous; it hides God as much as it reveals him. We do not find him in creation unless we have found him first in his active presence in history, in the experience here and now through his Word and his Spirit. As one of the important results of higher criticism, we know that Israel's confession of Yahweh as the Creator of the whole earth came after and because of her encounter with him in his liberating acts from the Exodus to the conquest of the Promised Land; and that this confession was made explicit in the Exile, by Deutero-Isaiah and the Priestly Writer, in their clash with the Babylonian creation-myths. Now that we know God in his mighty acts in history, we can recognize his actions also in his work in creation and preservation. We understand that the same God in action, the same *ruach* working in the deeds of salvation, is also the secret of the entire created world. The Old Testament is aware, even more than the New Testament, of the work of the Spirit in creation. We are inclined to begin with Genesis 1:2: ". . . the Spirit of God was moving over the face of the waters," but this translation is too doubtful to allow any consequences for our theme.[1] The main pronouncements we find in Job and the Psalms. The fact that we often are inclined to translate *ruach* in these texts as "breath" does not diminish their pneumatological value, as we saw in Chapter I. For the faithful Israelite it was clear that "By the word of the LORD the heavens were made, and all their host by the *ruach* of his mouth" (Ps. 33:6). Word and Spirit both describe God in action. God's Spirit creates and sustains the life of *nature:* "When thou sendest forth thy Spirit, they are created; and thou renewest the face of the ground"[2]; and particularly the life of *man:* "The Spirit of God has made me, and the breath of the Almighty gives me life."[3] So intimate is the Spirit to man's life that we sometimes feel ourselves on the brink of pantheism. Job says that he has the Spirit of God in his nostrils.[4] Nevertheless, in his immanence this Spirit remains strictly sovereign and transcendent. We cannot dispose of the Spirit within us. God gives his Spirit; he also takes him away, in which case man and nature die away. "If he should take back his spirit to himself, and gather to himself his breath, all flesh would perish together, and man would return to dust."[5] The Spirit of God also inspires man's *culture*. The Old Testament connects him with agriculture, architecture, jurisdiction, and politics (Cyrus as God's anointed one!). In general all human wisdom is the gift of God's Spirit.[6]

This relation between the Spirit and creation is much neglected in Christian thinking. Calvin and, following him, Abraham Kuyper are the only ones I know who tried to do justice to this cosmic aspect of pneumatology.[7] This neglect is deplorable for two reasons. First, because the special operation of the Spirit in the New Testament is presented as the restoration and fulfillment of his work in creation, and therefore is described in terms borrowed from his work in creation, like "vivify," "birth," "regeneration," "new creation." The outpouring of the Spirit is not an incident; as well as the Son, the Spirit "came to his own home." Therefore, we are encouraged to discover his traces with joy and gratitude everywhere in our created world. We must even say that only he who knows God's Spirit in re-creation can truly distinguish his signs in creation.[8]

A second reason for emphasizing this viewpoint is the fact that it can make the Spirit's work more relevant to many to whom the word "spirit" does not mean much. We all are sustained by the Spirit in every moment. He is as near to us as our life, our breath, our vitality, our mind, our creative gifts. The famous medieval anthem *Veni Creator Spiritus* is an excellent expression of the unity of the Spirit's work in creation and redemption:

> *Imple superna gratia*
> *Quae tu creasti pectora.*

And:

> *Infirma nostri corporis*
> *Virtute firmans perpeti.*[9]

DIVINE SPIRIT AND HUMAN SPIRIT

The Holy Spirit is "as near to us as our mind," we just said. It is this aspect of his presence in the created world which has drawn the special attention of many theologians since the rise of German Idealism. This partly results from the fact that in many languages the Holy Spirit and the human spirit are called by the same word ("spirit," "esprit," "Geist," "geest"). This gives the impression that we must define both in mutual analogy and that the human spirit, in a specific sense, is the entrance-gate and the dwelling place of the divine Spirit. This linguistic fact should not mislead us, however. The English language is better off than many others in that it has words which distinguish between both. I am not thinking of the unfortunate words "Holy Ghost," which point exactly in the wrong direction and should disappear from the ecclesiastical language as soon as possible; but I am thinking of the English word "mind," which, as a parallel of "spirit," and at the same time reserved for man, helps us to see that God's Spirit and our spirit belong to different realities. This is in accordance with the usage in the New Testament, where *pneuma* usually means the Holy Spirit and his operations in human life, whereas the human spirit, except when *pneuma* is used in a few cases, is mainly called *nous*.[10]

These considerations admonish us not to exaggerate the much-discussed problem of the relation between the divine Spirit and the human spirit. The Spirit, as the source of our life in its totality, includes not only our mind, but also our body, our vitality, our emotions, etc. The mind can be the place where our rebellion against God is concentrated, and in that case it is even further removed from the Holy Spirit than any other part of our nature.

This cannot be our last word, however. The "spirit" terminology is rather confused in our modern languages as well as in Hellenistic Greek. Apart from indicating the higher capacities of human nature, the word "spirit" can also have a more inclusive significance, so that it indicates our ego, the core of our personality, that which, in the Bible, is often called "heart." If we stick to this meaning, the problem of the relation between God's Spirit and ours becomes relevant anew. Is not our spirit in that case the point of contact and the dwelling place of the Holy Spirit? In this connection many appeal to Paul's words that "the *pneuma* himself bears witness with our *pneuma* that we are children of God" (Rom. 8:16). We press these words too far, however, if we read here some sort of *analogia entis.* The verb *summarturein* means that God's Spirit bears witness to our self in such a way that this self can no longer remain merely passive, but feels urged to support and to transmit this witness.

If our ego is a creature of God's Spirit, and if we are created in God's image, we must assume that there is a certain kind of analogy between the nature and the function of our ego and of God's Spirit. This problem is a part of the large and complicated problem of the relation between God's revelation in Christ and our created human reality. More than the European mind, the Anglo-Saxon mind is inclined to seek and to formulate this relation. Continental theology, insofar as it refuses to pay attention to this basic relation, is threatened by abstractness and sterility. Church and theology are bound to seek such a presentation of God's revelation that its relevance for our human existence and realities may become clear. We reject Marcion's separation between nature and grace. Every element of God's revelation presupposes that he comes "to his own home." Anglo-Saxon theology constantly puts this fact before us, as a confession as well as a theological program. On the other hand, European readers are inclined to ask whether this scope does not jeopardize the presentation of God's revelation in its sovereignty over and its tension with our human reality. The search for a relation between God's Spirit and our spirit can easily seduce us to an interpretation of the Holy Spirit in terms of the human spirit, which means: in terms of recent anthropological and psychological opinions. This starting point prevents many from taking into account that the gospel "is not according to man," nor to what "the heart of man conceived." It is often overlooked that the search for similarity is misleading if it does not help us also to see the dissimilarity between the content of our spirit and the content of the Spirit's judging and saving work. The search for similarity cannot produce more than formal results, discovering analogies in terms of structure, like: responsibility, communication, relation, personality, etc. As soon as it goes beyond that, it becomes arbitrariness or is in danger of blurring the distinction between God and man.[11]

We limit ourselves to the statement that the Spirit comes to his own home and that therefore we must assume an analogy between his works in creation and re-creation, but that we are unable to describe this relation in relevant terms. We do not know whence the Spirit comes and whither he goes.

Because our starting point for a doctrine of the Holy Spirit was Jesus Christ as the bearer and the sender of the Spirit, we did not pay much attention to the operation of the Spirit in ancient Israel. In the context of this chapter, we must deal with this theme. Israel belongs to the field of God's special revelation, but occupies a kind of middle position between creation and Christ, so far as pneumatology is concerned. God's deepest meaning with Israel was that in his gracious covenant relation with Israel the nature of created and fallen manhood might be revealed in such a way that the necessity of incarnation and atonement might become evident.

Only if we put the relation between Israel and Christ in this way can we understand the way in which the Old Testament speaks about the work of the Spirit in connection with the covenant. In this chapter we learned that Job and the Psalms speak about the Spirit in terms of creation; in Chapter I we learned that the later prophets speak about the Spirit in terms of consummation. Our question here is if and how the Old Testament speaks about the Spirit in terms of the present. The question must be answered in the affirmative, but the "how" differs widely from what we read in the New Testament. The Spirit dwells not in all the faithful, but in some chosen ones: the leaders during the Exodus and the entrance into Canaan, the judges, the kings; in Joseph and Daniel; and in a very specific way in the prophets.[12] The communion of the Spirit with the nation as a whole and with its individual members is reserved for the future. Often Psalm 51:11 is considered as an exception, where David prays: "take not thy holy Spirit from me"; but even here he prays as a king, who is conscious that he has sinned against his anointment with the divine Spirit. God's Spirit in ancient Israel is mainly the power which inspires and strengthens the organs of his covenant-revelation. Israel itself, as the partner in

the covenant, does not yet partake of this indwelling of God. God
and his partner stand over against one another. That is of the essence of the old covenant. Here it has to become evident that man
is even unable to be the obedient partner of the gracious God.
Here it must become clear that mankind needs a God who even
fulfills the role of his partner and who in a new covenant writes his
will upon their hearts (Jer. 31:31-34). For that reason the Spirit
operated in the covenant-organs. He worked also in the faithful
believers of the Old Testament, as a signpost toward the great
future; but the Old Testament avoids the word "Spirit" in this
context. The main impression is that the overall operation of the
Spirit in man will be the gift of the Messianic time and that, until
that moment, God withholds his Spirit, so that the necessity of a
new and deeper condescendence may become evident. The Old
Testament as a whole confirms the words of the Gospel of John:
"as yet the Spirit had not been given, because Jesus was not yet
glorified" (7:39).

THE SPIRIT IN THE PROCESS OF CHRISTIANIZATION

Now Jesus is glorified and his Spirit, according to the prophet
Joel, is poured out upon all flesh. This is even more true than we
Christians are inclined to believe. We confess that the Spirit is
operating on a world-wide scale in the churches and in the missionary movement, but at the same time we limit his operation to
the faithful church members and to the converts of the mission.
Contrary to this opinion, I believe that the impact of the Spirit as
the active presence of Jesus Christ in the world is far wider than we
are aware of.

According to the nature of the New Testament, we find in it
only some hints about this new relation of the Spirit to the world.
To make clear what I mean, I need more of a historical argument
than a biblical one. Christ said: ". . . make disciples of all nations
. . . teaching them to observe all that I have commanded you . . ."
(Matt. 28:19-20). Conversion means also the creation of a new
pattern of behavior, which in the long run influences the environ-

ment and transforms the social and cultural structures. The beginning of this process is found as early as the apostolic age. It is reflected in the domestic admonitions found in three places in the Epistles (Eph. 5:21—6:9; Col. 3:18—4:1; 1 Peter 2:18—3:7), where we read about the mutual behavior of husbands and wives, parents and children, masters and slaves. The authority of the Lord deeply influences the *married*, the *family*, and *social life* in terms of Christian love.

The next step was the refusal of the Christians to worship the emperor, which after a long period of persecution led to the de-deification of the *state*. As long as human societies had existed, they had rested upon the divine character of state authority. Now that this tradition was abandoned, the way was paved for influence of the people, independent jurisdiction, and democracy. When in the fourth century the Roman Empire became nominally Christian, a certain *Christianization of society* was inaugurated. Although the full display of this trend did not arrive until the Middle Ages, the ideal of an entire Christian civilization could be more or less fulfilled. This Christianization included the obligation of monogamy, the maintenance of Sunday, the protection of the church, and—as a clear break with the Roman traditions—the care for the oppressed, the helpless, the deprived. It is the gospel of Jesus which drew the attention of society to the *individual* and especially to the underdog. The same gospel helped the world after Christ to a sense of *history*. Before, the nations had conceived what we call history as a circular movement like the process of vegetation, or at any rate as an endless repetition of similar events. Now history is understood as meaningful, as governed by God and directed toward an end: the Kingdom of God. Christendom also introduced the concept of the *essential unity of the human race* as a consequence of the universal meaning of the incarnation.

Many, Christians as well as non-Christians, believe that this process of Christianization stopped in the periods of the Renaissance and the Enlightenment and was gradually replaced by a basically different process—that of secularization. This is a false opinion, however. Secularization is, in the first place, the continuation of Christianization. The difference lies in the fact that in modern times the consequences of the gospel are mainly drawn by those who are outside of the church and who are not aware of the source of their inspiration. These times are characterized by the discoveries of *science* and the inventions of *techniques*. The fact that Western Europe and North America were the bearers of this turbulent evolution was due to the fact that the demythologizing of nature had taken place in these areas in its most radical way. The old religions considered nature as the dwelling place of gods and demons; man therefore could not interfere with the natural processes without risking the divine wrath. Israel, on the contrary, believed that God was on the side of man over against nature and had called man to dominate nature in his name (Gen. 1:26-30; Ps. 8). Without this radical change in man's concept of nature, science, techniques, fight against diseases, etc., never would have taken place to the extent to which they have.

The consequences of secularism in *social and political areas* also have a Christian background. The gospel introduced a God who is not another name for the existing social order, but a revolutionary God, whose "righteousness" (*sedek*), according to the Psalms and the prophets, means that he lifts up those who are bowed down and humiliates the oppressors. He is the God who, with his laws of the Sabbath Year and the Year of Jubilee, checks poverty and pursues the equality of all his children. This new image of social standards is the primary source of our modern *revolutions,* in which again and again new groups of oppressed claim their rights. The French Revolution, with its ideals of liberty, equality, and fraternity, had far more to do with Jesus Christ than had those who resisted it in the name of Christ. After the French Revolution we witnessed the *emancipation* of the slaves, the women, the laborers, the colored races. Since the Second World War this revolutionary movement goes in an accelerated speed over the whole world. The liberating and transforming power of the Spirit of Jesus Christ is at work everywhere where men are freed from the tyranny of nature, state, color, caste, class, sex, poverty, disease, and ignorance. Eugen Rosenstock speaks in this context even of a biological change in man's nature. I prefer to speak of a pneumatological change. The age-old static structures of man's life with their dehumanizing effects are replaced by the transforming powers of the Spirit who, in the gospel, the mission, and the church, entered into our world and produces ever new consequences of God's message of liberation in the new man Christ.

This brief presentation of far-reaching thoughts inevitably evokes many questions and objections. Let me try to meet some of them in a few marginal notes.

1. All this does not mean that the Spirit of Christ created our modern culture out of nothing. Here as everywhere the re-creative work of the Spirit presupposes and uses his work in creation. The Greek philosophers, in particular, developed many insights about nature, state, the unity of mankind, etc., to which we owe much of our modern discoveries. However, these insights could not have borne fruits unless they were preserved in the Christian era as being akin to the Christian conceptions.

2. The question must arise: Why did so many of the fruits of the Spirit come so late, chiefly promoted by non-Christians and often resisted by Christians? Mankind lived in naturalistic patterns of life for thousands of years; small wonder that it took hundreds of years to draw the most radical consequences of Christ's dominion. The church herself by intuition did not welcome these last consequences. She was afraid that this emancipation of man would lead to the rejection of authority in general and would make him turn away from Christ to autonomy and nihilism.

3. The church was right insofar as she foresaw the fatal reversal of emancipation. She was wrong insofar as she tried to stop halfway the movement of the Spirit. The Spirit's work always has a double effect. He "is set for the fall and rising of many," "a fragrance from death to death" as well as a "fragrance from life to life." That holds good not only on the personal level but also on the cultural level. The Spirit's liberation can lead to reckless autonomy as well as to the acceptance of the Father of Jesus Christ as the Lord whom we in liberty have to serve. The church has to support the process of emancipation as much as she can; at the same time she has to preach the source and the meaning of this revolutionary movement.

4. The work of the Spirit in our modern so-called secularized world reminds us of the fact that our exalted Lord is not only the Head of his church but also primarily the Head of the world. The Spirit is not locked up in the church. We know that his work in the world is ambiguous; but so is his work in the church. Nowhere do we find him on earth in heavenly purity. In the faithful he raises the conflict between Spirit and flesh, in the world that between Christonomy and autonomy.

5. In spite of the deep shadows, the Spirit's work of humanizing men and their social structures is a parable, an analogy, and even a part of the great *summorphia* which has begun in Jesus Christ. It is a signpost toward the glorification of the universe, the conformity of mankind with its Head. As in the individual, it is not more than a small beginning. And this beginning is threatened by the fact that the majority of those who enjoy it do not know the center and the meaning of all this. They have the fruit without the root, the horizontal dimension without the vertical one. The church needs the instruction of the Spirit in world history in order to understand the cosmic consequences of her preaching. And the world needs the church to give meaning to its development, lest mankind's emancipation end in boredom and futility.[13]

THE ESCHATOLOGICAL CONTEXT OF THE SPIRIT

The fact that the relation of the Spirit to the great future is almost at the end of this book should not mislead us. The order of the subjects is not an order from higher to lower priorities. With equally good reason one can argue that this part is the most important because, according to the rule of logic: "what is the first in conception is the last in execution." Geerhardus Vos in his superb and still timely study "The Eschatological Aspect of the Pauline Conception of the Spirit" rightly says: "The Spirit's proper sphere is . . . the world to come; from there he projects himself into the present, and becomes a prophecy of himself in his eschatological operation." Alan Richardson in his chapter "The Holy Spirit" begins with a paragraph on "The eschatological character of the Spirit"; and Neill Q. Hamilton, writing on Paul's pneumatology, says: "The attempt will be made to show that the Spirit is related primarily to the future."[14]

This is in accordance with two facts already mentioned. First, the Holy Spirit is seen as the gift for "the last days," and these days have dawned in the resurrection of Christ and the descent of the Spirit. Second, the Holy Spirit is the exalted Christ reaching out to the *totum*, drawing wider and wider circles around the representative One, until the last goal is attained and *ta panta* are involved in the great renewal. For these reasons we can say that the Spirit, together with Christ, is the first fruits of the future and that at the same time he is preparing and reaching out to the consummation of the future which now has begun. We shall explain now what this means.

CHRIST, THE SPIRIT, AND THE CONSUMMATION

1. *Christ, the Spirit, and the consummation belong together.* As we pointed out before, Christ is the *pars* directed toward the *totum*, and the Spirit is he who leads from the *pars* to the *totum*. The Spirit is the movement from Christ to the consummation, from the first fruits to the full harvest. This is clearly expressed in the closing words of 2 Corinthians 3:18: We are being changed into Christ's likeness, which comes from the Lord who is the Spirit and which leads from one degree of glory to another, that is to say, to the full display of Christ's glory in his Kingdom, the *summorphia* of the whole creation with the new man.

Moreover: If Christ is the first fruits of the eschatological reality, then, consequently, the same holds true of all that results from his appearance, his work, and his resurrection. All these operations are "the powers of the age to come"; they all are summarized in the work of the Holy Spirit.

2. *In the work of the Holy Spirit the consummation begins.* This is first of all true in terms of justification. In faith and baptism the Spirit incorporates us into Christ's saving deeds: We die and rise with Christ, and we are made to sit with him in the heavenly places, elected as his fellow heirs and as adopted sons of God. Even more than justification, sanctification in the New Testa-

ment is considered to be the beginning of our glorification, the
prelude of consummation. To express this relation, Paul uses the
words *aparchè* and *arrabōn*. The first word reminds us of the Old
Testament laws about the first fruits of crop and cattle and even
man, which had to be sacrificed to God, as a token and a confession
that all that we have and that we are belongs to the Lord. The
usage of the word in the New Testament is slightly different. Here
the first fruits are not what we offer to God, but what he creates in
mankind; nor are they created in order that mankind as a whole
may be exempted from this dedication to God. But, on the contrary, they are a promise that the time will come when mankind as
a whole will be God's. The word *aparchè* is used for three realities:
Christ, the Holy Spirit, and the church. Christ as the new man and
his power to transform a community into his likeness are the first
fruits of the new humanity. In this connection the words in
Romans 8:23 are of special importance; Paul speaks here about the
church as "we ourselves, who have the first fruits of the Spirit."
The genitive "of the Spirit" is here doubtless a genitive of explica-
tion, so that we, with the N.E.B., can say: "we, to whom the Spirit is
given as firstfruits of the harvest to come." The Spirit, with all his
gifts of conversion, forgiveness, communion with God and joy in
him, is the first part of the coming glorification, the foretaste of the
Kingdom.

The same thought is in an even stronger way expressed in Paul's
second word: *arrabōn*. He borrowed this non-Greek word from the
Semitic business-language in the Near East (2 Cor. 1:22; 5:5; Eph.
1:14). The R.S.V. translates: "guarantee," the N.E.B.: "pledge." A
buyer who cannot pay the entire price at once gives an *arrabōn* as a
first installment, as a guarantee of his readiness to pay the whole
amount. Our nearest word is probably "down-payment"! God gives
his Spirit to his children as a token that his Kingdom is really at
hand, that he is ready to bring it.

In accordance with this conviction is the fact that the phraseology of the great eschatological events—the coming of Christ, the
resurrection of the dead, the judgment, the vision of God in Christ,
and the walking by his light—is also applied to the great pneumatological events. In the Spirit Christ's reappearance takes place
already; in him we rise from the dead, we are tested and judged,

we walk in the light of God's grace, and we see him through Christ.[15] The whole work of the Spirit (as well as that of Christ) is an anticipation of the consummation. The New Testament does not know a futuristic eschatology nor a realized eschatology but a realizing eschatology.

3. *The Holy Spirit makes us long for the consummation.* At first glance, this can seem to be in contradiction to the preceding point. At any rate, one is inclined to suppose that both points diminish each other's relevance; the more we experience the beginning of the future, the less we long for its total coming, and the other way round. This is not the New Testament view, however; here the experience of the future now and the longing for it are proportional to one another. We think anew of Romans 8:23. In verse 22 Paul said that the whole creation is groaning in travail; now he adds that the church also groans, i.e., "we . . . who have the first fruits of the Spirit." These words could mean: "in spite of the fact that we have the Spirit as the first fruits." However, a better explanation is: "because of the fact that we have the Spirit as the first fruits." We can best make this clear by a comparison with what often happens in our daily life. Someone who is ill can acquiesce in that situation as long as he is convinced that his disease is incurable; but, if a medical authority tells him that he can recover after a shorter or longer treatment, a new period of restlessness and longing begins. The more signs of recovery the patient discovers, the more his restlessness and longing grow. That is the paradoxical situation of God's children in the world. That they hope is not primarily due to what they miss, but to what they have already received. The joy and peace which are granted by the Holy Spirit make us abound in hope (Rom. 15:13). We have a hope which does not disappoint us, because God's love has been poured out in our hearts through the Holy Spirit which has been given to us (Rom. 5:5). Faith and love produce hope. In the light of what God has given, we discover how much the present situation of our world clashes with God's gifts in Christ and in the Spirit. That makes us look forward eagerly to a world which is re-created according to the gifts already bestowed upon us. In faith and hope we revolt against the status quo. The joy in what we possess evokes the groaning about what we do not yet possess. The experiences of

having and lacking keep pace with one another. They are one another's reversals in the fellowship of the Holy Spirit.

4. *The Holy Spirit is himself the content of the consummation.* This thesis is a direct consequence of the preceding paragraphs. If the Holy Spirit is the first fruits and the guarantee of the future, this must mean that the future will be in accordance with and of the same nature as that which we experience in the Holy Spirit here and now. The work of the Holy Spirit in our present age means that God claims our lives in a small beginning and that he, to the same extent, transforms our existence to the likeness of Christ. As a prolongation of this event, the consummation means that God will be everything to everyone, and that therefore our whole existences and our whole cosmos will be transformed to the likeness of Christ. We can define the consummation as the completion of the pneumatic process, as the full indwelling of the Spirit, as the "pneumatizing" of the whole creation. As a consequence, we, like Geerhardus Vos, have to say that the Spirit is the subject of the consummation.[16] When Paul speaks of the "spiritual body" which we shall receive in the age to come (1 Cor. 15:44), he does not think of a body made out of uncorporeal material (whatever that may be) but of a *soma*, a total human existence, soul and body included, which will be created, permeated, and controlled by the Spirit of Christ. And because Christ with his humanity is glorified, that is, partakes in the glory, the *doxa* of God himself, and because in Christ mankind has crossed the bounds which in creation were put between God and man—therefore the full indwelling of the Holy Spirit and our conformity with Christ will mean that, according to the bold words in 2 Peter 1:4, we shall "become partakers of the divine nature." In our present world we have no words or ideas to describe what that means, not even by analogy. It is enough to know that the power of Christ's resurrection, which is the power of his Spirit now in the world, is able to do far more abundantly than all that we ask or think. "Beloved, we are God's children now; it does not yet appear what we shall be, but we know that when he appears we shall be like him, for we shall see him as he is" (1 John 3:2).

VI

THE SPIRIT AND THE TRIUNE GOD

In many creedal statements and in most of the handbooks of dogmatic theology, much attention is given to the relation of the Holy Spirit to the Father and the Son in God's eternal trinitarian being. This is understandable in view of the age-long struggles in the ancient church concerning what we usually call the trinitarian dogma. In the Middle Ages this struggle was followed up by the conflict around the word *filioque* in the Nicene Creed, a conflict which resulted in the still unhealed split between the Eastern and the Western church. All this can well explain the traditional emphasis in pneumatology on the trinitarian aspect.

THE SPIRIT IN TRINITARIAN DOGMA

However, in this last chapter we shall not recapitulate this history and all the problems involved. The reader can find the data in the handbooks of systematic theology and of the history of doctrine. Moreover, I feel that this aspect in pneumatology has been overemphasized. When we think of the relation between the Spirit and the mission, his work in the world, the role of the spiritual gifts in the church—all themes which were entirely or almost entirely left out of systematic theology—we must admit that theology was far more interested in intellectualistic and speculative subjects than in those which could help the church and her members to see their role in God's great design. The Reformation opened a new field, the relation of the Spirit to the individual; this was real progress, but it did not diminish the emphasis on the traditional and more speculative problems. In addition to this, we must not forget that we have no "dogma of the Trinity" inherited from the ancient church, only some pronouncements of Councils about the divine character of Christ and of the Spirit. The formula "one being, three persons" from the very first moment left open several interpretations; even today it veils the problems instead of solving them. Finally, we may wonder whether all the traditional problems in this field can be considered as real problems from an existential point of view. I think mainly of the conflict around the *filioque*: whether the Spirit proceeds from the Father *and* the Son, *filioque*, or, as the Eastern church maintained, from the Father *through* the Son, *dia tou huiou*. In this conflict, motives of prestige and power-politics played such a dominant role that today many Eastern as well as many Western theologians feel unhappy about the either-or into which their church was formerly pressed.[1]

All this does not mean that the trinitarian thinking of the ancient church has no use for a sound doctrine of the Holy Spirit. On the contrary, the result of this thinking is still relevant today, insofar as the divinity of the Spirit is concerned. Many theologians of the second and third centuries were inclined to think of Father, Son, and Spirit in terms of subordination, according to the triadic and emanatistic Hellenistic philosophy of their day. As a consequence, especially in the theology of Origen and his school, the Spirit occupied the lowest place in the divine hierarchy, near to the spiritual realm of the created world. So the Spirit in the minds of many Christians was not more than a vague semi-divine cosmo-logical power whose main virtue was that it completed the divine Trinity. The fourth century brought a radical turn. Athanasius, the same man who attacked every conception of the Son as being a lower entity than the Father, drew the consequences of his position also for the conception of the Spirit. In his *Four Letters to Serapion* (358-362) he argued that because of his divine work the Spirit must be of divine nature. "If the Holy Spirit were a creature, we would have no fellowship with God in him; in that case we would be connected with a creature and we would be alien to the divine nature, so that we in no sense would have fellowship with it."[2] The other strong defender of the Godhead of the Spirit in that century was Basilius the Great in his book *The Holy Spirit* (A.D.

375) and in other writings. He uses basically the same reasoning as Athanasius. In one of his letters he writes: "You say that the Holy Spirit is a creature. Now every creature is the servant of the Creator. For he says: All things are thy servants [Ps. 119:91]. If the Spirit is a servant, he has holiness by obtaining. All who have holiness by obtaining are susceptible to wickedness. But the Holy Spirit, being holy by nature, is called the source of holiness; therefore the Holy Spirit is not a creature. If he is not a creature, he is of one substance with God."[3] The struggle and the victory of these Fathers is still relevant. If the Spirit is not God himself, but something less, he cannot reconcile us to God nor re-create us according to the image of the Son. In that case our redemption can only be expressed in terms of semi-Pelagianism, of a deeper knowledge, or of a moral improvement.

THE SPIRIT: THIRD PERSON IN THE TRINITY?

As soon as it was generally accepted that the Spirit is of one substance with God, the question arose as to what quality (the Greeks said: *idiotès*) distinguishes the Father, the Son, and the Spirit from one another. It is typical for Athanasius that he was not interested in this question and had no word for the innertrinitarian distinctions. Western theology, on the contrary, already had a long terminological tradition. Since Tertullian, in the Latin-speaking church the formula "one substance, three persons" (*una substantia, tres personae*) was commonly accepted. What does "person" mean in this context? Originally it meant the mask which the actor in the theater wore to indicate his role. The next significance was: the role itself, which led to a more general meaning: the role or function which a man performs in his social context. Finally, it came to mean: man's character. In theological terminology, *persona* meant at any rate more than an external mask or a mere function, but less than what our word "person" contains. It was a vague word which became a source of embarrassment and confusion for many centuries.

In the Greek-speaking half of the church, the three so-called

"Cappadocians," Basilius the Great, Gregorius of Nazianzus, and Gregorius of Nyssa, hammered out the trinitarian terminology for the coming generations. They could not translate the Western formula; *persona* is in Greek *prosopon*, which has a mere external meaning: "mask," "face," and does not bear the connotations of the Latin equivalent. In the ears of the Greeks this terminology would sound like the heresy of Sabellius who denied the essential distinctions in God. Basilius made a distinction between two words which until that time were used as synonyms in philosophical language, i.e., *ousia* and *hupostasis*. The Cappadocians spoke of the triune God as three *hupostaseis* in one *ousia*. The Latins, in their turn, could not translate this formula. The translation would be: *una essentia, tres substantiae*. In the ears of the Latins this terminology would sound like the heresy of three gods, tritheism. What it meant to the Greeks is not quite clear. Is Lossky right in thinking that *hupostasis* covers our modern notion of person?[4] Or does it have the same meaning as the ancient concept of individual substance? Is *ousia* meant as the ontological unity which embraces the three hypostases? Or is it used here as class-name, indicating the general nature which the three hypostases have in common? It was the latter significance of which the Latins were afraid, and not without reason. Basilius wrote: "The difference between *ousia* and *hupostasis* is that between the common and the singular, just as between the living being and the concrete man."[5] And Gregorius of Nyssa argued that the belief in the Trinity keeps the middle road between the pagan error of polytheism and the Jewish error of sheer monotheism.[6] Nevertheless, the Cappadocians tried to maintain the unity with the Latin part of the church. Gregorius of Nazianzus purposely puts the words *hupostasis* and *prosopon* together, saying: "We shall in no way quarrel about the names, as long as the words point to the same notion."[7] From the Western side, Hilarius, bishop of Poitiers, tried to interpret the Cappadocian presentation to the Latin-speaking theologians. So the difference in conception and terminology did not lead to a split. However, the consequence was that the concepts of "being" and "person," which until today form the skeleton of the doctrine of the Trinity, are open to more than one interpretation.

In the Western church, the confusion around the person-concept even increased in the following centuries. Augustine wrestled heavily with the terminology. He preferred the word *persona* to the word *substantia*, but he was not satisfied with it either. His are the famous words: "When one asks: what three?, the human speech suffers of a great lack of power. Nevertheless, we say: three persons, not in order that we would say this, but that we would not be silent."[8] The reason for Augustine's special embarrassment was the fact that he introduced a new conception of the Trinity in which Father, Son, and Spirit had lost all substantial distinction and had become relations within the one Divine Being. They are related as memory, intellect, and will are related within the mind; or as in love: the lover, the object of love, and the act of love. Especially this last image is dear to Augustine; "so there are three: the lover, that which is loved, and love."[9] In Augustine's doctrine the term "person" is, properly speaking, more fit for the triune God than for the three relations within him. The Spirit is, even more than Father and Son, a mere function, as he is the act of love, the bond which connects the Father and the Son.

In the next century, through the famous and influential definition of "person" by Boetius (*rationalis naturae individua substantia*), a less vague and more "dense" person-concept was introduced, even further removed than the former one from the Augustinian idea. Small wonder that Augustine's followers could now do even less than the master with the word "person." Anselm of Canterbury was afraid to speak of "three persons" in the sense of "three substances"; therefore, he speaks of "three I do not know what."[10] And Thomas Aquinas argues that "person" cannot mean anything else than "relation," though a relation "which is its own mode of being" (*ut subsistentem*).[11] The Reformers were even less interested in the terminological heritage of the ancient church. Calvin derides those who speak of the Trinity in analogy to "three men" and even more those "who under the papacy had the audacity to delineate three little men (*trois marmousets*) *et voilà la trinité*."[12] Calvin's own definition is: " 'Person,' therefore, I call a 'subsistence' in God's essence, which, while related to the others, is distinguished by an incommunicable quality."[13] This definition can represent many other Lutheran and Reformed descriptions of the person-concept.[14] The persons in the Trinity are considered as being different ways in which the one Divine Being exists, *modi subsistentiae* or *modi entis*. This is still the position which is represented in many textbooks. The word "person" is maintained but used in a sense which widely differs from the content which it has today.

This scholarly tradition did not penetrate to the man in the pew, however. He heard of the "first," the "second," and the "third" Person of the Trinity and he understood this "person" in accordance with the common European person-concept, i.e., as a center of self-consciousness and self-determination. Therefore, his trinitarian conception was and is still far nearer to that of the Cappadocians than to that of Augustine. With the restriction that it is doubtful whether he "understood" the Trinity in this way, or did not understand it! Most Christians accept the traditional doctrine of Trinity only with a more or less avowed sacrifice of their intellect—unless they are simply tritheists.

The cleavage between the theological and the present usage of the word "person" has not left the doctrine of the Trinity untouched in the long run. Since the end of the eighteenth century, we have witnessed a kind of cult of "the person" who now condenses to "personality" (*Persönlichkeit*), to an autonomous and self-conscious power which by its moral strength defends itself against the impersonal powers around. Schleiermacher understood that this modern concept was not applicable to the Holy Spirit. He saw the Spirit as the *Gemeingeist*, the continuous influence of Christ on the church, which unites and inspires the community.[15] Modernism in the nineteenth century broke with the person-concept and, following in the line of Schleiermacher, considered the Spirit as the name for the deep and steady influence which the doctrine and the example of Jesus still exercise in the hearts and lives of innumerable people, an influence higher than, but not essentially different from, the influence of other religious or cultural personalities and trends.

The adherents of the orthodox tradition in the church were aware that something was wrong, when the Spirit was treated as an impersonal force, as a "something" between God and Christ, on the one hand, and the church and the individual, on the other. Therefore, the Evangelicals introduced as a feature of orthodoxy the slogan "the personality of the Holy Spirit." They wanted to maintain the direct and personal relation between God and the individual as well as the sovereignty of the Holy Spirit in the work of regeneration. Their purpose was sound, but their slogan meant the casting out of the demon by Beelzebul. In order to save the sovereignty and the personal character of the Spirit's work, they introduced the modern concept of "personality," with all its connotations of autonomy. This concept must inevitably lead to some kind of tritheism. Modernism was right in that it rejected this person-concept in pneumatology. Even less than in former times did the word "person" really express the relation between the triune God and the Spirit. Nevertheless, the confused and confusing phrase "the three persons of the Trinity" is still used. It is no use to maintain it any longer, especially since this formula from the very beginning has functioned not as a power of unity but as a source of confusion.

THE RELATION BETWEEN GOD, CHRIST, AND THE SPIRIT

We have even more reason to say farewell to the person-concept in pneumatology. We learned in Chapter I that the word "Spirit" is basically a predicate to the nouns "God" and "Christ," and that modern biblical theology has made clear that in the New Testament the Spirit is the name for the exalted Christ acting in the world. The image which arises out of the biblical studies is about this: God is a living, acting God. In creation he transmits his life to a world outside of his being. In the act of creation, he therefore becomes a life-giving Spirit. As Spirit he sustains and develops his created world, he elects and protects Israel, he calls and governs her leaders and prophets. In the fullness of time, God himself becomes man. Incarnation is the highest act of his Spirit. From now on the world has the center of God's activity in its midst. Jesus Christ is the acting God present in our world. God's Spirit from now on is

Christ's Spirit, without ceasing to be present in a more general way in the created world. God's action in the exalted Christ is his more specific operation, in the light of which his general operation is revealed in its ultimate meaning. Christ as Spirit permeates and sanctifies the created world, until all things are summed up under Christ as their Head and mankind is re-created according to his image.

What we see before us in biblical revelation is a great divine movement, the movement of God as Spirit, moving toward the Son and out of the Son. It is a movement which urges us to utter three words: God-Christ-Spirit, or according to the order of our experience, as H. P. van Dusen did in his book: Spirit-Son-Father. These three names in their togetherness point to a movement of the one God, not to a static community of three persons. They are the description of an ongoing movement of condescendence, in which God reaches out deeper and deeper toward man in his sin and distress, until in the end he can touch the heart of the individual by his regenerating power in the Spirit of Christ. Then the Spirit leads man to Christ, and in Christ man finds God. So we must recognize a double movement: God stretches out his arm and his hand toward his fallen world and next draws man up toward himself, to press the prodigal son to his heart and to grant him the transformation according to the image of Christ.

In all this God is Person, acting in a personal way, seeking a personal encounter. The triune God does not embrace three Persons; he himself is Person, meeting us in the Son and in his Spirit. Jesus Christ is not a Person beside the Person of God; in him the Person of God becomes the shape of a human person. And the Spirit is not a Person beside the Persons of God and Christ. In creation he is the acting Person of God, in re-creation he is the acting Person of Christ, who is no other than the acting Person of God. Therefore, we must reject all presentation of the Spirit as an impersonal force. The Spirit is Person because he is God acting as a Person. However, we cannot say that the Spirit is a Person distinct from God the Father. He is a Person in relation to us, not in relation to God; for he is the personal God himself in relation to us.[16]

Therefore, the three names in the New Testament: God

(Father)–Christ (Son)–Spirit are not meant to express a kind of tripartition in God, which would distinguish the Christian faith from Jewish monotheism (an old misunderstanding, still alive). On the contrary, in using these three names together the Apostles want to confess the unity of God, the fact that in the great movement of Spirit, Son, and Father we have not to do with three entities, but with one and the same acting and saving God. Take, for example, the closing words of 2 Corinthians: "The grace of the Lord Jesus Christ and the love of God and the fellowship of the Holy Spirit be with you all." It would be in contrast with the whole trend of Paul's thinking if we would assume that grace, love, and fellowship (koinōnia, the communication of the gifts of the Spirit) are three different realities, given by different entities. Grace, love, and communication are three ways of describing God's one saving work. Accordingly, Jesus Christ, God, and the Holy Spirit are three ways of describing God's one saving reality. We have to do here with a kind of Hebraic parallelism, serving to suggest the movement and variety which are inherent in the work of salvation. The same parallelism is found in the triadic sentence in 1 Corinthians 12:4-6.[17]

Nevertheless, we can and we should not oppress the question which occupied Christian theology from the beginning: How can we understand this plurality in God's creating and re-creating activity as being consistent with biblical monotheism? It is doubtful whether we have conceived of this monotheism in the right way. Even the Old Testament does not preach a God who is numerically one. The Hebraic word for God, Elohim, is plural. In some cases this God speaks about himself in the plural (Gen. 1:26; 11:7). He holds judgment "in the midst of the gods" (Ps. 82:1). On the one hand, he is transcendent above all creatures; on the other hand, he (so to speak) reduplicates or even multiplicates himself in the intercourse with his people. We think of his name, his Word, his face, his Spirit, his angel. He is "Yahweh of Hosts," surrounded by heavenly powers who carry out his decrees and in whose activities he himself is present and acting. God in the Old Testament is a communion within himself, an organism, a unity in diversity, as G. A. F. Knight states clearly in his remarkable

study "A Biblical Approach to the Doctrine of the Trinity."[18] This
plurality and diversity of God have to do with his activity and with
his condescendence. He is a moving God; he is a movement of love.
Such a movement cannot be described in one word or in one name.
God's being toward us cannot be expressed, so to speak, in a
picture, only in a film. Against this Old Testament background, the
trinitarian phraseology of the New Testament is nothing revolutionary. As Yahweh, the transcendent God, nevertheless dwelt with
his people in his name, his face, his Spirit, so he is now present in
his Son and in his Spirit. They are not other Gods, nor are they
other departments within one Godhead. They are the same God,
now present and active in a new way, multiplicating himself without dividing himself, expressing his unity in a plurality.

Now we have to come back to the classical dogmatical terminology. In Western theology we found three main ways of expressing the distinctions within the Trinity: *persona, subsistentia* or
modus subsistentiae, and *modus entis*. We saw why the word
persona is useless. The word *subsistentia*, used by Thomas Aquinas,
Calvin, and their followers, was more abstract and less "heavy"
than "substance." It pointed to a reality, which though being a
relation, is more than a quality (*accidens*), because it is characterized by the fact that it has its own mode of being. To us the
word *subsistentia* as meaning something between *persona* and
substantia is no longer valid. The only expression which can satisfy
us is *modus entis*, "mode of being," used by several theologians in
the period of Reformed scholasticism.[19] It is a modest word, which
cannot create tritheistic misunderstandings, but at the same time,
it makes clear that God does not exist in one way, but in different
ways. He expresses the unity of his being in a diversity of ways.

Here the question arises whether we should not prefer to speak
of *modi revelationis*. We know that God reveals himself as Father,
Son, and Spirit; but are we allowed to conclude from that fact the
mystery of God's being itself? Would not that be a bad kind of
speculation? My answer is that, according to biblical thinking, to
make separation between God in his revelation and God in his
eternal being would, on the contrary, be speculative. We have
nothing to do with a nature of God outside his revelation. We may

believe that he is as his revelation is. Otherwise his revelation would not be a "re-vel-ation," an "unveiling," but a veiling. In the way in which God acts in his ongoing condescendence toward man, he reveals his deepest nature. With Paul we may ask: "Who has known the mind of the Lord?" And with Paul we may answer: "But we have the mind of Christ" (1 Cor. 2:16), which means: in the mind of Christ, revealed to us by the Spirit, we have access to the inaccessible mind of the Lord. That entitles us to speak not only of modes of revelation but of modes of being.

This fact has far-reaching consequences. It means that the history of God's condescendence is not only a history for men but also a history within God himself. His movement is not outside of himself. He is himself involved in his own movement. He himself is the movement. Knight dares to say: "God has gained something throughout the centuries as a result of what has happened in the sequence of time; God has himself grown in experience as a result of his gracious love for man." This is a risky way of theologizing. Two pages later Knight has to tone down his statement by saying: "God grows and yet does not grow."[20] Nevertheless, at any rate, we must ask: Can we prevent ourselves from believing that God himself will be enriched when in the consummation, as a result of his double movement of condescendence and elevation, his prodigal son will be brought home to participate in his glory?

I know one theologian who has tried to project a doctrine of the Trinity strictly from the viewpoint of this double movement. His name was Marcellus, bishop of Ancyra, who lived in the fourth century. At first he was a friend of Athanasius, who defended his strange conception of the Trinity. He was heavily attacked by Eusebius of Caesarea, and after his death, he was condemned as a heretic. His central category was, according to the terminology of his time, that of logos, by which he understood God in action. The Logos, according to Marcellus, was resting within God until he appeared as "activity" (in Greek: energeia) in the creation. That was the first "dispensation" (Greek: oikonomia). The second was the incarnation, in which the Logos was even separated from God, because of his unity with the human flesh. The third dispensation was the going out of the Spirit on Pentecost. In all these three activities the one God maintains his unity. What happens is a successive extension (Greek: *platunesthai*) of God's activity. Because this extension takes place in time, it will also have an end. The Logos and the Spirit will return to the inner life of God, so that the position before creation will be restored.[21]

We know Marcellus only from fragments, quoted and attacked by his adversaries. Therefore much is unclear to us. We understand that he was condemned because he taught that 1 Corinthians 15:28 had to be understood as the ending of Christ's dominion and existence. He could not imagine that the history of salvation would be of eternal relevance to God as well as to us. Nevertheless, in that decisive century in which the concept of the Trinity was hammered out for the coming ages, he was the only one who understood this theological task in its full biblical extent. More than the others, he was initiated into biblical thinking. He saw that the Logos as well as the Spirit is God himself in a special activity. He saw also that Scripture is not interested in the God of an abstract eternity, but in the God who acts in time and history. That inspired him to his bold concept of God's trinitarian extension in history. So he made a radical attempt to historicize the theological categories. His tragedy was that he was not radical enough. He limited the trinitarian extension to the present *oikonomia*. He felt urged to dehistoricize God's being in the eschaton. So he offered a welcome point of attack to his adversaries who did not understand him.

We still have a long way before us until we shall have a new common doctrine of Trinity which will help our church members instead of confusing them. This time I believe the renewal will not come from a discovery of the biblical content of the word *logos* (as in the days of Athanasius and Marcellus) but from a discovery of the biblical content of the word *Spirit*.[22] This is a notion which appeals to modern man and (what is more) which by its biblical meaning has the possibility of freeing our conception of God from the static, abstract, and unhuman elements which, in the view of so many, are still inherent in it. God is Spirit! The Lord is Spirit! That means: They are seeking us, saving us, elevating us. God is a moving God who wants to bring us into motion toward our eternal goal. He seeks us in the Son; he reaches us in the Spirit; he brings us by the Spirit to the Son and in him to the Father. "I believe in the Holy Spirit" means: I believe in a God who is involved in a double movement in which he involves his church, the world, and also me.

Notes

CHAPTER I

1. F. W. Dillistone, *The Holy Spirit in the Life of Today* (Philadelphia: The Westminster Press, 1947), p. 25.
2. Alan Richardson, *An Introduction to the Theology of the New Testament* (New York: Harper & Row, Publishers, 1958), pp. 104-105.
3. Karl Barth, *Kirchliche Dogmatik* (Zürich: EVZ-Verlag, 1940), II, 1, § 31, 1, p. 541. English translation, *Church Dogmatics* (Edinburgh: T. & T. Clark, 1957), p. 481.
4. George S. Hendry, *The Holy Spirit in Christian Theology* (Philadelphia: The Westminster Press, 1956), p. 32.
5. *Epistle to the Magnesians*, 15.
6. *2 Clemens* IX, 5.
7. *Pastor Hermae, Similitudo* V, 6, 5. This passage and its surroundings are often misunderstood as adoptionistic. So does Harnack, who nevertheless considers the general trend of the primitive pneumatic Christology to be anti-adoptionistic. He is in danger, however, of reading these texts from the standpoint of later controversies. See *Dogmengeschichte*,[4] I, pp. 182 ff. A more adequate presentation is found in the superb study by Arnold Gilg, *Weg und Bedeutung der altkirchlichen Christologie* (reprint of 1936), München: Kaiser Verlag, 1961.
8. Tatianus, *Adversus Graecos Oratio*, 7.
9. John Calvin, *Institutes of the Christian Religion* (Philadelphia: The Westminster Press, 1960), Book Three, I, 1, pp. 537-538.
10. Barth, *op. cit.*, IV, 1, § 62, 1, p. 724; English translation, p. 648.
11. See, e.g., Eduard Schweizer, article *pneuma* in *Theol. Wörterbuch zum N.T.*, VI, pp. 394-449; Ernst Käsemann, "Geist und Geistesgaben im N.T.," *R.G.G.*,[3] II, col. 1272-1278; Neill Q. Hamilton, *The Holy Spirit and Eschatology in Paul* (*Scottish Journal of Theology*. Occasional papers 6), Edinburgh: Oliver and Boyd, 1957; Ingo Herrmann, *Kyrios und Pneuma. Studien zur Christologie der paulinischen Hauptbriefe*, München: Kösel Verlag, 1961; Kurt Stalder, *Das Werk des Geistes in der Heiligung bei Paulus*, Zürich: EVZ-Verlag, 1962.

12. Herrmann, *op. cit.*, p. 140.
13. *Ibid.*, p. 57.
14. Calvin, *op. cit.*, Third Book, I, 1, p. 537.
15. Käsemann, *op. cit.*, col. 1274.
16. Herrmann, *op. cit.*, p. 58.
17. This last sentence is very similar to the words used by Stalder, *op. cit.*, p. 54 (in his paragraph on "Das Pneuma und der Kyrios"). However, on other pages Stalder is more inclined to assume a certain duality between Christ and the Spirit (e.g., p. 61).
18. In Calvin we find already a tendency, though weaker, to identify the work of Christ in his pre-existence, as well as after his resurrection, with the work of the Holy Spirit. The exalted Christ is absent so far as his human nature is concerned; he is present in his divine nature, i.e., in his Spirit. (This separation between the two natures is not tenable, however.) See Werner Krusche, *Das Wirken des Heiligen Geistes nach Calvin* (Göttingen: Vandenhoeck und Ruprecht, 1957), pp. 24, 140-151.
19. Barth, *op. cit.*, IV, 2, § 64, 4, pp. 360, 361; English translation, pp. 322-323. This sudden widening of Barth's pneumatology was less unexpected to himself than to his readers. Even in the passage of IV, 1, § 62, 1, which we mentioned as being typically traditional, Barth says that he limits himself purposely to the awakening power of the Spirit. "To that extent we have not yet said of Him everything that there is to say."

CHAPTER II

1. Harry R. Boer, *Pentecost and the Missionary Witness of the Church* (Franeker: T. Wever, 1955), p. 12.
2. They thought of words like Ephesians 6:17; Hebrews 4:12; and 1 Peter 1:23.
3. They thought of words like Matthew 11:25; 16:17; Luke 24:45; Acts 16:14.
4. Barth, *op. cit.*, IV, 3, § 71, 4, p. 651; English translation, p. 567. See all of § 71, 4, "The Christian as Witness."

CHAPTER III

1. Augustinus, *Sermo* 267, 4.
2. See the paragraphs 424, 697, 799, 930, 964.
3. The quotations are from the sections II, 2, b, and II, 3, Preface.
4. The quotations are from the parts I, B, 3, c, and II, 1.

5. A. M. Henry, *l'Esprit-Saint* (Paris: Librairie Arthème Fayard, 1959); see particularly ch. 7.

6. Emil Brunner, *Dogmatik III* (Zürich: Zwingli Verlag, 1960), ch. II, 1, p. 34. English translation, *Dogmatics* (Philadelphia: The Westminster Press, 1962), p. 19.

7. H. Bavinck, *Gereformeerde Dogmatiek*, Vol. IV² (Kampen: J. H. Kok, 1911), p. 357.

8. I point especially to the first half of this booklet, called *The Divine Trinity and the Unity of the Church* (London: SCM Press Ltd, 1960).

9. O. Noordmans, *Liturgie* (Amsterdam: U. M. Holland, 1939), p. 72.

10. The Westminster Press, 1942. I quote from the second edition (1944), pp. 74 and 76.

11. I found this translation in F. A. Cockin, *God in Action* (London: Penguin Books, 1961), p. 66.

12. Jean-Louis Leuba, *l'Institution et l'Evénement. Les deux modes de l'oeuvre de Dieu selon le Nouveau Testament, leur différence, leur unité* (Neuchâtel-Paris: Delachaux & Niestlé S. A., 1950). I quote from the last and concluding page, 124.

13. *The Body. A study in Pauline Theology* (London: SCM Press Ltd, 1st ed., 1952).

14. "*Vos estis quod accipitis,*" *Sermo* 227.

15. George S. Hendry, *The Holy Spirit and the Renewal of the Church*, in *The Bulletin Moravian Theological Seminary*, Bethlehem (Pa.), Fall 1962, p. 29.

16. We may add that as from a dogmatical point of view the institutional work of the Spirit is neglected, so from a practical point of view we discover the opposite neglect. For in spite of our theory, our church institutions are often very massive and authoritative and the "priesthood of all believers" is more an ideal than a reality. As Dr. Henry P. van Dusen writes, the institutional aspect "will find adequate guardians in the Church, whose every instinct is for their preservation. . . . The great need of the Church is for precisely those gifts which can come to it only through the Holy Spirit in its creative and prophetic freedom." *Spirit, Son and Father* (New York: Charles Scribner's Sons, 1958), p. 144.

17. Hendry, *The Holy Spirit and the Renewal in the Church*, p. 30.

CHAPTER IV

1. Calvin, *op. cit.*, Book Two, II, 7, p. 264.

2. Canons of Dort, III/IV, par. 11 and 12.

3. In Greek the words are even stronger than we can express, because

Paul uses verbs with the preposition *sun*, which in literal translation would become: co-crucified, co-buried, etc. See Romans 6: 1-11; Ephesians 2:6; Colossians 2:12-13; 3:1.

4. For the Lutheran position, see *Apologia*, XII, 46; for the Reformed position, Calvin, *op. cit.*, Book Three, III, 8-9, pp. 632-634.

5. For Calvin, see *op. cit.*, Book Three, III, 8, p. 600; for the common opinion, Heppe, *Die Dogmatik der evangelisch-reformierten Kirche*[2] (Neukirchen: Neukirchener Verlag, 1958), chapter *De sanctificatione*, especially pp. 449-450 and pp. 455-456.

6. See Romans 6:6; Ephesians 4:22; Colossians 3:9. For the reason mentioned in the text, the translation "old nature" and "new nature" (R.S.V., N.E.B.) is incorrect. It obscures the christological meaning. Paul knew how to distinguish between "man" (*anthropos*) and "nature" (*phusis*). In Romans 6:6 the translations "our old self" (R.S.V.), "the man we once were" (N.E.B.) are good.

7. See 2 Corinthians 4:7-17; 6:4-10; also 1:8-10; 11:23—12:10; Romans 8:35-39.

8. Both quotations are from Hermann Friedrich Kohlbrugge's *Questions and Answers for Clarification and Confirmation of the Heidelberg Catechism*, the first in the section on Q. 75-79, the second in the section on Q. 60. (I quote from the Dutch translation, 4th ed., Amsterdam, n.d.).

9. See Calvin, *op. cit.*, Book Three, XIV, 14, 18-20; pp. 784-787; Wilhelm Niesel, *Die Theologie Calvins* (München: Chr. Kaiser Verlag, 1938), pp. 162-173; S. van der Linde, *De Leer van den Heiligen Geest bij Calvijn* (Wageningen: H. Veenman en Zonen, 1943), pp. 148-149; Krusche, *op. cit.*, pp. 245-254. Krusche gives the most careful exposition of this theme.

10. For another exposition of this problem, see my article in *Essays on the Heidelberg Catechism* (Philadelphia-Boston: United Church Press, 1963), pp. 115-116.

11. Unless Max Weber is right when he tries to prove that in the rise of capitalism Calvinistic industrial effort, inspired by the *syllogismus practicus*, played a decisive role. This thesis is very doubtful, however.

12. An excellent exposition of the relation between faith and experience is given in the *Consensus Bremensis* (1595), VII, 5 and 6. (See E. F. K. Müller, *Die Bekentnisschriften der reformierten Kirche*, Leipzig: A. Deichert, 1903, pp. 758 f.)

13. The frequent use of this and similar expressions in the Lukan writings requires a special study which has not been written until now. See Luke 1:15, 41 ff., 67; 2:26-27; 4:1, 14-15; Acts 1:8; 2:4, 17-18; 4:8, 31; 6:3, 5; 7:55; 8:16-17; 9:17; 10:44-46; 13:9, 52; 19:6.

14. See Acts 11:28; 13:1 ff.; 15:32; 1 Tim. 1:18; 4:14. Also Acts 21:14; 1 Thess. 5:20.

CHAPTER V

1. Another possible translation is: "A storm of God (i.e., a heavy storm) was sweeping over the waters" (so, e.g., Martin Buber). In that case these words are an affirmation of the preceding words in verse 2, which describe the chaotic situation of the world. A third possibility, which appeals to me, is: "but the wind of God blew over the waters"; in that case God makes the chaos dry by a wind; cf. Exod. 14:21-22; Ps. 18:12-15; 104:7, etc., as an analogy of what he did in the deliverance of Israel. See J. H. Scheepers, *Die Gees van God en die Gees van die Mens in die O.T.* (Kampen: J. H. Kok, 1960), pp. 246-263.
2. Ps. 104:30; cf. Eccles. 3:19-21.
3. Job 33:4; cf. 32:8; Gen. 2:7; 6:3; Isa. 42:5.
4. Job 27:3.
5. Job 34:14-15; cf. 4:9; Ps. 139:7; Eccles. 3:19-21; Isa. 31:3; 40:7.
6. Agriculture: Isa. 28:26; architecture: Exod. 31:3; 35:31; jurisdiction: Num. 11:17; politics: Isa. 45:1-5; wisdom: Job 32:8; Dan. 1:17; 5:11.
7. For Calvin, see S. van der Linde, *op. cit.*, pp. 34-57. For Kuyper, see his *The Work of the Holy Spirit*, Vol. I, ch. II.
8. Cf. Gösta Lindeskog, *Studien zum neutestamentlichen Schöpfungsgedanken*, I (Uppsala-Wiesbaden, 1952), and Barth, *op. cit.*, III, 1, pp. 60-63; English translation, pp. 57-59.
9. My English translation, in *Cantate Domino*, does not express what is meant in these lines (as most translations fail to do). I translate literally: "Fill with thy celestial grace the breasts which thou hast created," and: "Strengthen perpetually with thy power the weaknesses of our body."
10. Even in the well-known words "the spirit indeed is willing, but the flesh is weak" (Mark 14:38), we have to write "Spirit" (with a capital S), because it is an allusion to Ps. 51:14 (see Kittel, *ThWNT*, VI, p. 394). Remarkable is Paul's distinction between *pneuma* and *nous* in 1 Cor. 14:14-19, where *pneuma* is the direct effect of the divine Spirit in man and *nous* the conscious mind which has to serve as an instrument to the operation of the Spirit.
11. To what different and often contradictory results the search for the analogy between God's Spirit and ours can lead, we see when we, e.g., compare three recent treatments of this subject: Arnold B. Come, *Human Spirit and Holy Spirit* (Philadelphia: The Westminster Press, 1959); Lindsay Dewar, *The Holy Spirit and Modern*

Thought (London: A. R. Mowbray & Co. Ltd., 1959); and George S. Hendry, *The Holy Spirit in Christian Theology* (London: SCM Press, 1957), ch. V: "The Holy Spirit and the Human Spirit." The first speaks in terms of communion, love, person; the second of the "hidden resources" of community and freedom, revealed in occultism and psychiatry; the third, in a more restrained way, in terms of freedom as man's lost relation to God.

12. I follow the list in the English summary in J. H. Scheepers, *op. cit.*, especially pp. 312-315.

13. For a deeper consideration of these questions, I refer to the German edition of my book *Der Sinn der Geschichte—Christus* (Göttingen: Vandenhoeck und Ruprecht, 1962), especially ch. V and the literature which is mentioned there.

14. Geerhardus Vos in *Biblical and Theological Studies by the Members of the Faculty of Princeton Theological Seminary* (New York: Charles Scribner's Sons, 1912), p. 228; Alan Richardson, *op. cit.*, pp. 105-107; Neill Q. Hamilton, *op. cit.*, p. 17.

15. See, e.g., John 5:25; 16:16-22; 1 Cor. 11:31-32; Eph. 1:18; 2:5-6; 5:15.

16. Vos, *op cit.*, pp. 225-235. Vos points to Rom. 8:11; Gal. 6:8, and especially to the role of the Spirit as the subject of Christ's resurrection (Rom. 1:4; 1 Cor. 6:14, etc.).

CHAPTER VI

1. For doubts about the Western position, see George S. Hendry, *The Holy Spirit in Christian Theology*, ch. II. An elaborate treatment of the problem is found in Serge Boulgakof, *Le Paraclet* (Paris: Aubier, 1946), pp. 87-143; Boulgakof speaks of "the dogmatical misunderstanding." It is significant that *Orthodoxy, A Faith and Order Dialogue* (Geneva: World Council of Churches, 1960) is silent about this problem.

2. *Epistula I ad Serapionem*, 24 (*Migne, Patrologia Graeca*, 26, 585).

3. *Epistulae*, n°8 (ad Caesarienses, anno 360), par. 10 (*Migne, P.G.*, 32, 261).

4. Vladimir Lossky, *The Mystical Theology of the Eastern Church* (London: J. Clarke, 1957), ch. III.

5. Basilius, *Epistulae*, n°236 (to Amphilochius, anno 376), par. 6 (*Migne, P.G.*, 32, 884).

6. In *Logos Katechetikos*, ch. III.

7. In *Oratio* 39, 11 (*Migne, P.G.*, 36, 345).

8. *De Trinitate*, V, 9. For the same subject see also VII, 4, where he even says (in par. 8): We use the expression "three persons" "not because Scripture does so, but because Scripture does not forbid."

9. Augustine, *op. cit.*, IX, 2, and *passim*. See also VIII, 10; and, for the *vestigia trinitatis* in general, VIII-XI.
10. *Monologium*, c. 78.
11. *Summa Theologiae*, I, quaestio 29, Art. 4; quaestio 30, Art. 1.
12. In *Congrégation de la divinité de Christ, Corpus Reformatorum*, XLVII, 473.
13. Calvin, *op. cit.*, Book One, XIII, 6, p. 128.
14. The Lutherans in general stress more the fact that the Trinity is beyond our understanding; the Reformers make more attempts to describe the mystery. The word *modus* is typical for Reformed theology.
15. See his *Glaubenslehre*, Vol. II, *passim*, especially §121-125.
16. Cf. Martin Kähler, *Dogmatische Zeitfragen*, II, 2nd ed. (Leipzig: A. Deichert, 1908), p. 214. To conceive of the Spirit as a person in relation to God, he says, would contradict the classical dogma of the Trinity (!) and "would express something which would have no importance for our faith in God." "On the other hand, of decisive importance for us and for our life in faith is the fact that God's Spirit is person *toward us* and that therefore in him God himself meets us in person."
17. See Ingo Herrmann, *op. cit.*, especially pp. 136-139.
18. G. A. F. Knight in *Scottish Journal of Theology Occasional Papers n⁰I* (Edinburgh: Oliver and Boyd, 2nd ed. 1957).
19. Wolleb and Keckermann use this expression literally; others use the Greek equivalent, introduced by the Cappadocians: *tropoi huparxeōs*. The word *modus* either in connection with *subsistentia* or without apposition is even more widely used.
20. Knight, *op. cit.*, pp. 61, 63.
21. The fragments of Marcellus are mainly preserved in Eusebius' two writings against Marcellus. They are collected in *Die griechischen christlichen Schriftsteller der ersten drei Jahrhunderte, Eusebius, Vierter Band* (Leipzig: J. C. Hinrichs'sche Buchhandlung, 1906), pp. 185-215. See especially the fragments 9, 14, 52, 60, 67, 70, 71, 77, 103, 113-117, 120, 121.
22. As a consequence of the insights here developed, I see the words *ruach*, and *dabar*, *logos* and *pneuma*, as synonyms. John's doctrine of the pre-existence of the *logos* points to the same reality as Luke's narration of the conception by the *pneuma*.